Our Last Season

Also by Harvey Araton

Driving Mr. Yogi

When the Garden Was Eden

Cold Type

Crashing the Borders

Alive and Kicking

Money Players
(coauthor)

The Selling of the Green
(coauthor)

Our Last Season

A Writer, a Fan,
a Friendship

HARVEY ARATON

PENGUIN PRESS

NEW YORK

2020

PENGUIN PRESS
An imprint of Penguin Random House LLC
penguinrandomhouse.com

All images not indicated below courtesy of the Musler family.
page 1, page 7 (top), and page 8: courtesy of the author; page 2 (top):
courtesy of the *New York Daily News*; pages 3 and 4: © Eileen Miller.

LIBRARY OF CONGRESS CATALOGING-IN-PUBLICATION DATA
Names: Araton, Harvey, author.
Title: Our last season : a writer, a fan, a friendship / Harvey Araton.
Description: New York : Penguin Press, 2020. | Includes index. |
Identifiers: LCCN 2019053128 (print) | LCCN 2019053129 (ebook) |
ISBN 9781984877987 (hardcover) | ISBN 9781984877994 (ebook)
Subjects: LCSH: Araton, Harvey. | Araton, Harvey—Friends
and associates. | Musler, Michelle, 1936–2018. |
New York Knickerbockers (Basketball team) | Sportswriters—United
States—Biography. | Basketball fans—United States—Biography. |
Basketball—New York (State)—New York—History. | Friendship.
Classification: LCC GV742.42.A77 A3 2020 (print) |
LCC GV742.42.A77 (ebook) | DDC 070.4/49796—dc23
LC record available at https://lccn.loc.gov/2019053128
LC ebook record available at https://lccn.loc.gov/2019053129

Printed in the United States of America
1 3 5 7 9 10 8 6 4 2

Designed by Amanda Dewey

For Beth, of course

Contents

INTRODUCTION

Ad-libbing

September 2017

All too well, my wife knew the pattern, and it meant trouble. After more than three decades of living with a man also married to his work as a reporter and newspaper columnist, she recognized distraction that was quickly devolving into full-blown obsession.

The closer we got to the critical day, the more unsettled I was getting. Dread was a state I hadn't yet reached, but with each fitful night's sleep, I suppose I was getting there, too. Finally, Beth had had enough of what one might call conversations in which I apparently hadn't listened to a word she'd said. You're being honored at the Hall of *freaking* Fame, she told me. You need to figure out a way to relax and enjoy this, not drive yourself and everyone around you crazy about making a damn speech.

"So do yourself a favor," she said. "Call Michelle."

Call your friend, your career adviser, your unpaid therapist. Dial her long-memorized 203 area code number—Stamford,

Connecticut—and talk it out, as you've done so many times before.

Call Michelle.

For almost four decades, I had been doing that, reaching out to the steady voice of reason in my life, the proverbial wise elder, the trusted friend I always could count on. We all need one like Michelle Musler, whose instincts and insights and tough but dedicated love had guided me through so many professional and personal storms. In the parlance of basketball, the game we loved and shared, she was the coach who knew how to help me be the best version of myself.

As a player, I maxed out my abilities as a five-foot-eight, shot-happy and turnover-prone point guard at a Jewish Community Center. Only in my most grandiose adolescent fantasies as the second coming of "Pistol Pete" Maravich or Walt "Clyde" Frazier could I imagine myself as a Hall of Famer. Nonetheless, I was headed to the Naismith Memorial Basketball Hall of Fame in Springfield, Massachusetts. Named for the legendary sportscaster Curt Gowdy, the award I was about to receive was actually for watching from the sideline, an honor bestowed annually on one member of the print media and one from the broadcast side for distinguished coverage of the sport. *That* connection to the game I could make without mocking realism or risking conceit. I dearly loved basketball and had dedicated a great deal of my four-decade-plus career to chronicling it for four newspapers, the past quarter century as a columnist and reporter for the *New York Times*.

The award came with a trophy and a fine-print inscription on a wall of past winners inside the shrine for the actual greats, from George Mikan to Michael Jordan. But it required doing what I enjoyed least: talking in public about myself, in this case addressing a dinner crowd of several hundred that would include:

The woman I had been married to for thirty-two years. The boys we had reared to young adulthood. An assortment of talented colleagues. Men and women—from David Stern to Bernard King to Dwyane Wade to Geno Auriemma to Rebecca Lobo—whose celebrated careers I had regularly chronicled and critiqued. Rare in a life of sixty-five years is a gathering so inclusive—except, I suppose, one's funeral. But from the time I was notified of the Gowdy Award in February 2017, I found myself trying to minimize it, half joking that I must not have insulted or alienated enough people within the basketball establishment that would grant such an honor.

My young-adult sons, in whom I had instilled a love of the game, wouldn't hear it, disabusing me of that self-shielding sentiment with their enthusiasm and pride. For no better reason than it was so important to them, it had to be for me, as well. And the closer it got, the more significant the award seemed to become, and the more anxious I was. In the days before the event, I compulsively fine-tuned my speech as if the Pulitzer Prize were hanging in the balance. I wanted it to be smooth, entertaining, a story in itself. Of course, manic rewrites were nothing new for me; they were now a familiar, if still unpleasant, part of my established writing process.

I doubt that many would have characterized me as shy, even noticeably modest. I was just always most comfortable and happiest in front of a keyboard, alone with my words and my whims.

And while I'd had some experience speaking to audiences for one professional reason or another, I just never fancied the spoken word as my strength, the spotlight as my friend.

The speech was formatted to be no longer than five minutes, though I'd been told by prior winners and a few basketball officials not to worry if I exceeded the requested limit. (Just avoid Peter Vecsey territory, they said. A onetime colleague of mine at the *New York Post*, in 2009 Vecsey had droned on for roughly half an hour before no less a luminary than Jordan walked out, music was queued, and the mic was cut.)

Given that precedent, I actually wasn't too concerned about the length of my speech. But I had been forewarned that there was to be no teleprompter, as there would be the following night at the nationally televised show for the induction of players and coaches. Naturally, I didn't want to read the speech at the expense of eye contact with the crowd. Nor did I want to lose my place and stutter myself into a state of babbling incomprehension. Hence, my nerves. Falling asleep, I had visions of fumbling the papers while the crowd murmured uneasily and my embarrassed sons slouched in their seats. Practicing in front of Beth—each attempt short-circuited by a glitch that elicited convulsive laughter or a string of profanities—was driving us both nuts.

So I took her sound advice. I called Michelle, who began by telling me to relax; I would be fine no matter what. She also knew me well enough to guess that such a promise was a waste of her breath. An hour later, an email landed—in all uppercase letters, as were all of Michelle's messages, legibly shouted to get my attention.

HARVEY . . . WHY NOT TRY REDUCING YOUR SPEECH TO BULLET
POINTS . . . AND PRACTICE WITH JUST THAT OUTLINE INSTEAD OF
TRYING TO READ & LOOK AT THE AUDIENCE . . . IT MAY JUST
SOUND . . . MORE SINCERE.

Great idea, I wrote back. And got right to work, grateful as always that Michelle, who had made her living managing and coaching corporate executives, was always happy to hear from me and to help. During my years at the *Times* and for most of my days in the newspaper business, I had covered all sports, traveled around the world, shared great adventures with too many bright, talented people to count. But there was no one quite like Michelle. No smarter friend. No better mentor. At the crossroads and crises of adulthood, there was no wiser and more trusted elder. Her little speech tip was but a tiny example of the times she had been a lifesaver for me in a multitude of more challenging life crises. I owed her so much.

"Come to the Hall of Fame dinner," I had told her weeks before, knowing that without her it would not be complete.

"That's a time for you and your family," she said.

"You *are* family."

"I know, but you know what I mean," she said.

I did. I also knew that wasn't the real reason why, at eighty-one, sixteen years my senior, she declined the invitation.

My brief time in the Hall of Fame spotlight began awkwardly, those seemingly endless few seconds of unfolding sheets of paper on which the speech was printed, complete with bullet points. I looked uneasily into the crowd, glanced to my left, to the table where my family was watching. *Please don't botch this*, I begged myself.

I talked about coming of age in New York when the iconic basketball figures were Willis Reed, Walt Frazier, Dave DeBusschere, Earl Monroe—the championship Knicks of the early seventies. I transitioned to covering the Dream Team in 1992, starring Michael Jordan, Magic Johnson, and Larry Bird. I don't remember the exact moment I began to relax and even enjoy my five-plus minutes of so-called fame. Michelle's suggestion of bold-faced bullet points no doubt helped the flow of the speech, allowing me to improvise and feel at ease in the moment and especially to enjoy the part I had looked forward to most: a few lighthearted but loving words in tribute to Beth and my sons, Alex and Charly. Momentarily, my mind wandered: Was I missing anyone else? It hit me in a flash, more nearly egregious oversight than epiphany.

> *Over the years, at four newspapers, I've had so many great colleagues: reporters in the trenches, editors who mentored and put up with me . . .*

And one remarkable, irreplaceable woman I managed to ad-lib into my speech, in the nick of time:

> *Michelle Musler—a special lady who's been sitting right behind the Knicks bench for the past forty years. My de facto career coach.*

Only those in the crowd who were regulars at Knicks home games would have recognized the name, or grasped why I had singled her out. I was just relieved to have avoided an omission that would have gnawed at me for the rest of my life. The following day, I eagerly sent Michelle a link to a video of my speech. She wrote back not long after, still digitally shouting:

> YOU DID A GREAT JOB. AND I THOUGHT YOU LOOKED TERRIFIC TOO. I LOVED MY MENTION—YOU WERE RECOUNTING YOUR ENTIRE CAREER AND YOU TOOK THE TIME. THANK YOU! I SAID, WHOA, I FEEL LIKE I ALSO MADE THE HALL OF FAME!!!!

Those who knew Michelle, who had in one way or another shared their love of the game with her, would have unanimously agreed: In the pro basketball annals of Madison Square Garden, in the history of the Knicks and their most devoted fans, she was one of a kind. In my life, she held the same hallowed place.

One

Homecoming

The instant I steered into her narrow driveway, Michelle emerged from the front door of her row-house condo and pulled it shut behind her. She was more than ready to go. She was raring. The Garden—and another game—beckoned.

It was a few minutes after four on a gray, misty Friday afternoon in Stamford, Connecticut, a few weeks after my Hall of Fame induction, a new NBA season underway. We were headed into Midtown Manhattan, to a Knicks game, not unlike any of the thousands we had attended—Michelle, the fan, in her choicest of locations in the first row right behind the Knicks bench, and I, the journalist, nearby in a courtside press seat.

Madison Square Garden was the center of our sporting universe, the footing on which our friendship was founded. Over the years, we shared our love for the game—however abysmally played by the Knicks—but on that October night, days before Halloween, it had a measurably different feel, an unmistakable sense of denouement. Any game we attended together at this point in time was conceivably our last.

A fixture for decades behind the Knicks bench, Michelle was no longer a season-ticket holder. She had them for this game against the Brooklyn Nets thanks to the largesse of a wealthy financial mogul who, for several years, had been her semisecret benefactor. The tickets had once actually been affordable—a bargain, even. For years, Michelle had owned four, selling off the two that were nearby in her section, on the railing a few feet to her right, and using the markup to help defray the cost of her own seat. But courtside prices surged with the NBA's popularity, growing steeper by the season. Michelle held on to her remaining life luxury for as long as she could, while admitting, "I'm embarrassed to tell people what I pay for basketball tickets."

Finally, the realities of retirement and living on a fixed income set in. In 2011, when the Garden underwent an expensive redevelopment, the price of a single-game seat for Michelle soared from $330 to $900 per game. There was an option to move to a cheaper location, away from the court, far from the action, back to where she had started many years earlier. She wasn't interested, admittedly spoiled. She figured she was done—until Wynn Plaut, the financier, stepped in to keep her in her seat, in the game.

Plaut's wife, Robin Kelly, was a friend of Michelle's from their yoga class in Greenwich, just south of Stamford. Even there, basketball was a uniting force. The studio was run by the wife of Gail Goodrich, a Hall of Fame player from the sixties and seventies, who occasionally showed up to fake his way through the routines, happier to talk hoops with Michelle.

Plaut's parents were dying. His son had cancer. His marriage was in jeopardy. His wife had gone to a few games with Michelle and had enjoyed the scene. He thought, *OK, these are really expensive but I'm in the financial world; I've done fine. Maybe going to some games with Robin might reconnect us.* The marriage didn't survive, but Michelle somehow managed to become a confidant to both as they hurtled toward divorce—and she continued attending games with one or the other.

Michelle, the Knicks loyalist, was the true survivor. Her arrangement with Plaut allowed her to attend her fair share of the season's forty-one home games. But she was pushing eighty and winter night driving had become an adventure best avoided by the 2016–17 season. She went from rarely missing a game to needing someone—usually Plaut—to give her a ride.

For several years, she had promised him a time when she would step aside and he could have the tickets, for which he was paying roughly a hundred thousand dollars, transferred to him. That time arrived with the renewal for 2017–18, along with a sad realization. "It gets to a point where you have to just accept that you're *old*," she said. "But to be honest, when I began thinking I couldn't go anymore, it made me so depressed because being in those seats has been my identity for so long."

I knew what she meant. I, too, was in a quasi state of withdrawal, having taken a buyout in the fall of 2016 from the *Times*, having convinced myself, only months from my sixty-fifth birthday, that it was my time to slow down, engage the world differently: resume piano lessons I had abandoned twenty years earlier; volunteer in my community; spend more time with family and friends; liberate myself from the never-ending demand for content and the inherent loneliness of being with a laptop. All easier said, or imagined, than done. Three weeks after leaving the *Times* staff, I was back to contributing as a freelancer on a fairly regular basis, weighing in on the Knicks, the NBA, and assorted other subjects. As it turned out, I hated the sound of the R-word. I winced whenever Beth would use it in reference to me in conversation with friends. I settled on telling people I had only *downsized* my career, not retired entirely.

Nor did Michelle have to completely detach herself from courtside at the Garden, thanks to Plaut's continued generosity. About the time he took full possession of her seats, he had bought a place in Florida, and was planning to spend more of his winter there. He had taken on a partner to share in the cost of the tickets, but told Michelle there still would be games available to her. She mentioned to me on the phone in early October that Plaut was more than offering; he was *pressuring* her to take him up on the offer. "Probably because he knows how painful it is for you to have given them up the first place," I said.

She sighed, admitted that she would of course love to go if only she could figure out a way to get there. I told her I'd be happy to take her.

"You'll come all the way up here, go into the city and then back up?"

"Why not?"

Michelle protested my having to do all that driving—just not vociferously enough to convince me that she wanted me to rethink the offer. We set our date for a game against the Brooklyn Nets. An email from Michelle arrived the next day.

ARE YOU SURE?

I was more than sure. I was thrilled. And nobody had ever had to twist my arm to go to a game and sit in a courtside seat.

We pulled out of her driveway, cruised through the streets of downtown Stamford and onto Interstate 95—as usual, slowed to a truck-infested crawl.

"I have to tell you, this is so exciting for me . . . because my life has become so *fucking* narrow," Michelle said as a sixty-minute ride into the city stretched in traffic to ninety.

I stole a glance at her—dress stylishly casual, hair meticulously done, makeup carefully applied. Still elegant. But noticeably struggling with her new terms of engagement. A proud woman well known to her friends for refusing to stay in her lane, becoming more and more dependent on the kindness of others.

Finally reaching Midtown, we turned onto Thirty-fourth Street and pulled into her regular indoor garage. Michelle exited the car as the elderly often do, in slow-motion stages. The parking attendant greeted her with a hug before steering my car into an easy-access spot obviously reserved for a VIP—who clearly wasn't me.

At the cashier's window, the face of the woman who took my payment lit up when she noticed who was beside me.

"Michelle!" she said. "So good to see you."

I could see that Michelle was pleased by the attention, especially with me as a witness. But it was nothing I hadn't seen before. Everyone in or around the Garden seemed to know her.

We proceeded into the arena and up to the glass-enclosed Delta Sky360 Club, a posh mélange of food and drink stations for owners of the priciest season tickets. When the club originally opened following a renovation of the self-proclaimed World's Most Famous Arena, I wrote a column about the dilemmas for longtime Knicks courtside ticket holders created by the exorbitant price markups. Michelle already had struck her arrangement with Plaut, but some of her oldest Garden friends had left, and others, in seats farther from the court, no longer had access to the same club. Michelle was more than annoyed. She was offended. "They've segregated the damn sections," she complained, not relishing being in a first-class cabin that was off-limits to those in coach.

Once-unimaginable price escalation was destroying what had been a sense of family and community. She could at a moment's notice drop a half dozen names of the dearly departed. More and more in recent years, there were nights when Michelle had felt practically anachronistic, a distant alumnus returning for a homecoming game.

Inside the club, she looked around and saw only unfamiliar faces. She'd been hoping that Walt Frazier and a few of the other former players who often made the social rounds would come by. But no one so much as acknowledged her until a young woman named Dani Brand, the Garden's consumer service representative for elite ticket holders (official title: premium experience specialist), came over to give her a hug.

"I feel a bit like a stranger in here now," Michelle told her.
"No way—this is your second home," Dani said. Not really, Michelle knew. Not so much anymore.

She had tried to be pragmatic and unemotional about the deal with Plaut. But surrendering her tickets had been an agonizing capitulation to age, a disengagement from the place that made her feel different, unique. She had dreaded the nights ahead at home, the television close-ups of the Knicks bench, wondering whose faces—if not Plaut's—might peek through the gaps between the players and coaches, in *her* seats. She knew the partner he had taken on—a young entrepreneur named Noah Goodhart—and liked him very much. She still worried that her tickets would wind up being used as symbols of privilege more than passion, as business bargaining chips. "That's driving me crazy," she said.

This for years was a chronic Michelle complaint: fans who weren't *real* fans, just those with the financial wherewithal and access, more into what the NBA branded its *in-game experience* than the actual game. To Michelle, these embellishments amounted to continuous noise that served as a wily NBA marketing scheme: a potent distraction from hearing oneself think about how much was being spent on those nights when the game was poorly played or hopelessly lopsided. Or—as was too often the case in recent years—when a superstar or two was conspicuously missing with a hastily contrived medical condition that amounted to a night off to rest. "The real fans," she said, "don't need to sit there and watch someone ride a unicycle balancing dishes on his head."

The more expensive the tickets became, the more *pretend* fans there were, taking selfies, scoping out celebrities—some of whom were comped their seats for the very purpose of being eye

candy. When someone at the Garden would point out a celebrity—
an Ethan Hawke, a John Turturro, a Woody Allen—she had a
standard reply: *Big deal.*

Who would come to a basketball game to watch *other* people
watch the game?

Having finished our dinner in the club, we made our way out
to the court, Michelle carefully navigating the narrow pas-
sageway between the team bench and the front row. I followed
close behind and stopped when she paused to greet Jonathan
Supranowitz, the Knicks' director of public relations.

A Brooklyn boy, Supranowitz was the media director in an
organization dominated—all but destroyed, as many Knicks fans
would argue—by James Dolan, scion of the Cablevision family
dynasty. The working conditions at the Garden under Dolan,
who held the same regard for most newspaper reporters as does
Donald Trump, had become, at best, barely tolerable. Some of
the beat writers believed that Supranowitz relished enforcing
Dolan's Kremlinesque rules—ordering staff to restrict access to
players while eavesdropping on whatever interviews were allowed, among other degradations.

Michelle was well aware of Dolan's petty media feuds—his
staff went so far as to keep dossiers on reporters covering his
basketball and hockey teams. Reporters for the *Daily News*,
whose coverage of his chronically losing team Dolan deemed too
negative, were never called on at news conferences or were
locked out entirely. But Michelle liked Supranowitz and was of
the mind that he was just doing—or protecting—his job.

Tall and lanky as some of the players, he had grown up a devout Knicks fan during the mideighties, and beyond. At home games, he liked to chat up fans before getting on with his night's work. Michelle, he said, was a star attraction, the regular he most enjoyed seeing, night after night, waiting for her to appear with a small token of his appreciation.

In the days when the media sat courtside, with beat reporters or star columnists usually positioned to the left of the bench, a stack of media game notes would be placed on the table by the seat reserved for the public relations director. Michelle—and only Michelle—helped herself each night to a packet, page upon page of statistical minutiae she would seldom look at, until the game notes vanished along with the reporters.

"Where did the stats go?" she asked Supranowitz.

"The media doesn't sit here anymore," he told her.

"Well, *I* do," she said.

Fair point, he thought. From then on, he made sure to hold on to one packet, reserved for Michelle, when she emerged from the club—not that she needed it. If she read anything before a game, or at halftime, it was a newspaper—the *Times* or one of the city's tabloids she lugged around in a tote bag embellished with an embroidered *M*. Yet Michelle gratefully accepted the game notes, brought them home, dropped them onto a shelf. She had stacks and stacks, just part of her ever-expanding collection of Knicks and NBA memorabilia saved over decades. Posters, books, photos of her with various Knicks personalities, framed newspaper clippings that detailed—humorously, in some cases—her basketball fanaticism.

She had long been a hoarder, unable to part with her kids'

baby clothes and furniture, until she bought her condo and sold her family home in 2004 and nearly drove herself crazy confronting the mountain of *stuff* in her garage. She hired someone to help her sort through it all and part with much of it. Her basketball collection, including every Knicks yearbook over twenty-seven years, went with her.

Supranowitz smiled when he saw Michelle coming his way, walking stiffly through the aisle. He had noticed that she hadn't attended any of the preseason games or the home opener against the Detroit Pistons a few days earlier.

"Where ya been?" he said, handing her the game notes.

"Well," she said apologetically, "I've had a couple of little strokes."

He nodded. "No excuses," he said.

She didn't argue with him. I almost suspected that she agreed. *No excuses.*

For as long as I had known Michelle, only the rarest of occasions counted as a rationale to miss a Knicks home game. A crucial work trip. A child's illness. During one extended spell, over the course of roughly a decade, she missed a single regular-season home game. And God forbid she not show up for a playoff game—though that hadn't been a problem of late, as the Knicks had seldom qualified for the postseason in recent years.

Few would dispute Spike Lee's status as the Knicks' most famous and visible fan, preening in the superdeluxe seats across the court from the bench on Celebrity Row. But to her way of thinking, Michelle was more symbolically situated—happily and partially hidden, right *behind* her guys. "Like Dani said, this has been my second home," she said wistfully as we settled into our seats.

Now she, too, was just a visitor, having moved on, like so many others long ago priced out—or aged out, if not carried out. Only a few of the section's regulars—Bob Iger, the executive chairman and former CEO of the Walt Disney Company, to name-drop one—could afford to show up on the occasion of a visit by LeBron James or Stephen Curry, while passing on the majority of game tickets to family, friends, or business contacts.

Change had become the norm at the Garden for Michelle, accelerating like the passage of years. Weeks after this night's game against the Nets, even Supranowitz would no longer be around to greet her and hand her the stats when—or if—she showed up next. He was laid off by a new Knicks management team, replaced by someone who would not know her name, much less her history.

"It's a strange feeling to be sitting here now," she said.

I felt a surge of emotion, put my arm around her, and snapped a selfie of us with my phone.

"For me, too," I said.

J ust a few feet away from Michelle's seats had been my station for multiple decades, a privileged courtside perch on press row. No more, though. Not for several years. First had come a move to a newly carved-out press section several rows behind one of the baskets and then a veritable banishment to the arena's second-highest level, far above where sneakers could be heard squeaking on hardwood floors, above other sweet sounds and sights of the game. The seats from which reporters could really see the game, bring it to life for their readers, were now packaged with waiter service for the corporate elite and one-percenters.

To reporters half my age, recollections of being close enough to the action to hear what the players and coaches were saying were akin to my admission of lugging around a portable Olivetti typewriter during my earliest days covering the Knicks in the late seventies. I might as well have admitted to reaching the Garden by horse and buggy. But I had to admit it was a treat to be courtside again, to experience the game as I once routinely did, even if a security guard always seemed to be blocking my view into the Knicks' team huddle. Was it my imagination or a deliberate House of Dolan obstruction of a nosy media member appearing where he wasn't supposed to be?

Like the rest of the fan base, neither Michelle nor I had great hopes or expectations for the 2017–18 season. The Knicks had already lost their first three games, two by routs. Michelle was nonetheless happy because Carmelo Anthony, a player she disdained, had been traded to Oklahoma City before the start of training camp. After six-plus seasons, the Knicks had finally moved on from the failed experiment of a one-dimensional gunner as their franchise star. They were now committed to rebuilding around the intriguing Kristaps Porzingis, a twenty-two-year-old, seven-foot-three, multiskilled skyscraper from the basketball hotbed of Latvia. Having watched Porzingis closely the past two seasons, Michelle was high on him as the team's future. She said he also seemed to be more aware of his surroundings, more cognizant of the fans, unlike many of the younger players of the past few years.

"He's a throwback, like some of the players from the eighties and nineties," she said.

"You mean he's acknowledged you?" I teased.

"Oh, yes, a few times, nods and smiles," she said. She insisted the attention was not the point—though I knew that wasn't completely true—but more symbolic of a player who wasn't self-involved, who understood what it meant to play for the Garden's ever-hopeful loyalists.

Being able to make such judgments was one of the great benefits to sitting behind the bench, Michelle had always maintained. In her prime, or when the Knicks had a roster that wasn't as transient as it had been in recent years, she could have written her own book on the behavioral character of the coaches and players.

As the game began—the Knicks promptly falling behind an equally youthful, inexperienced Brooklyn squad before rallying to take the lead in the second quarter—Michelle was distracted by an unfamiliar middle-aged man sitting immediately to her left. She knew he was a problem right from the start. Whenever play moved to the far side of the floor and something of note occurred—a dunk, a blocked shot, a hard foul—the man would stand up, blocking her line of vision and making a spectacle of himself. He did this repeatedly until she'd had enough. When he next stood up, she yanked on his elbow, trying to pull him back down. He didn't budge, or seem to notice.

"Did you just grab that guy?" I said.

"I did," she said. "I'm going to punch him next time. You paid all this money for a seat. *Sit* in it!"

I was strangely heartened to see that Michelle, bless her, hadn't lost her feistiness.

At halftime I wandered off to say hello to Cal Ramsey, who was perched a short distance away alongside the ramp, where Michelle had once sat—back then an excellent spot to chat up reporters as they breezed by on their way to press row. Ramsey was a former New York University star who played briefly for the Knicks in 1959 before falling victim to early NBA racial quotas. During my years on the beat and beyond, he had been a broadcaster, a community relations specialist, and a friend to the franchise heroes Willis Reed and Earl Monroe, among many others.

Players came and went, but people like Ramsey and the longtime photographer George Kalinsky gave the Garden its warmth, its charm, its pulse. So many others—men like John Condon on public address; the timekeeper Nat "Feets" Broudy; the old championship coach, Red Holzman—had passed on. With every departure, Michelle felt another block removed from the foundation of the life she had built for herself at the Garden. As did I.

Now the wheelchair-bound Ramsey was failing, health issues having begun during the summer when he fell out of bed, cracked open his head on the edge of a table, and needed twenty-five stitches to close the wound. While hospitalized, tests revealed trouble with his heart, a trace of cancer. After we chatted, I promised myself that I would double back soon to interview Ramsey for the kind of column—what a pair of ancient eyes saw in Porzingis and these young Knicks—more easily conceptualized from courtside than from our sequestered enclave high above the court. When I told Michelle that chauffeuring her to the game had provided the gist of a column, she smiled.

"You don't have to convince me that this is where *something* was always happening."

I agreed, and told her that covering games at the Garden had never been the same after we had moved upstairs.

"Now you're starting to sound like me, an old fart," she said.

You might say. Except in Michelle's case, I would have better characterized her as an esteemed Garden loyalist, and part of its greatest generation.

Two

. . . .

The Making of a Fan

Michelle's kid brother bristled the day she dared show up to watch him shoot baskets with friends on a cement playground in working-class Hartford, Connecticut. Robert Bassell, not quite two years younger than his sister, stared her down, then finally yelled out, "What are you doing here?"

"I like to watch," she said, defending her right, refusing to budge, giving birth to a long life of basketball spectatorship and, more significantly, holding her own in strategic conflict with men.

Her brother died in 2012, but late into life, Michelle and Robert—Uncle Bob to her five kids—would routinely and affectionately *go at it* at family Thanksgivings, agreeing on little about the world and especially their childhood, save for the fact that Michelle was no conventional or ordinary girl. She had seemingly been born with a chip on her shoulder and a suspicion—if not an actual belief—that there had to be more to life than what was prescribed for a girl from a working-class family.

Michelle Frances Bassell, known in her early days as Mickie, had no use for "dolls and other girlie things." She was drawn to the games only boys played, even if there was no chance she could participate in them. She compensated by becoming the sports editor of her high school newspaper.

She persisted past those who implied that she was unfit for the role, though, using her considerable sports knowledge to convince skeptical male coaches to take her seriously, not treat her as *cute*. She remedied the problem of not having transportation to road games by going to the school principal and talking her way onto team buses. She covered all the major team sports, but basketball was the game she was drawn to. It was theatrical. It was vivid. Faces weren't hidden behind helmets or under caps; for spectators up close, players' expressions and emotions were practically matters of public record. "And that means you know them better," she reasoned.

Two decades before the championship Knicks owned New York, before I was even born, Michelle was already a courtside fixture, daydreaming of what was then an unattainable career. It would take another quarter century for women to bust through the sports-writing barricade—far too late for her.

The truth was that Michelle had no apparent path to *any* professional employment, or even to college. The daughter of a Jewish steam fitter and an Irish immigrant mother, she spent her earliest years in the Hartford projects until her father saved enough money to buy a modest home in a working-class neighborhood.

Blue-collar financial stability did not resolve old-world social disorder. Michelle grew to preadolescence without a full-time father, who kept his out-of-religion marriage—and two children—a secret to keep the peace with his mother. Until she died, Harry Bassell led a double life, dining with his family after a day of maintaining and repairing piping systems and leaving soon afterward to sleep under his mother's roof.

This continued for years, Michelle and her brother well hidden from their Jewish relatives. Her mother, Sarah, stayed home, sleeping late. Michelle remembered her hunched over a newspaper in the kitchen, seldom cheerful or communicative. In all likelihood, Michelle would guess decades later, Sarah was clinically depressed by the aberrant family circumstances, the faith and class distinction.

Adding to her disorientation, Michelle and her brother were sent to a Catholic elementary school, where she was called "Christ-killer" by classmates for being half-Jewish and targeted with other taunts and the occasional punch on the way home. After she complained to her mother, a priest sat her down and suggested she respond as a *good Catholic girl should—turn the other cheek*. Which exorcised any interest she may have had in religious education.

When the grandmother she never got to hug passed away, Michelle finally met her father's family when an uncle visited her home with his children. She immediately sensed the difference between these newly introduced cousins and those on her maternal side. They seemed *different*—more self-assured, yammering on about school, their favorite subjects, their plans for college. The more she was around them, the more she understood that for them, such a future was not even in question. She began for the first time to strongly consider that possibility for herself.

Soon freed from the horrors of parochial school, she set out on a mission at Bulkeley High School to be important, popular, high achieving. In addition to editing and writing sports for the newspaper, she was the lead in a class play. She was voted junior prom queen. She was popular with the boys. But then she was stricken with tuberculosis, placed into an upstate quarantine for months, the story of her illness covered in a Hartford newspaper. She would never forget the contagion unit, the glass wall, her teachers driving up to deliver reading assignments. Upon recovery, she returned to school and promptly discovered her popularity had expired.

"I was the girl who had TB," she said. "I became an outcast."

She switched her focus to college—taking two buses each way to a more upscale section of the city for math tutoring—but was rejected by the one school, William & Mary, to which she applied. It was senior year. Michelle was suddenly panicked by the thought of staying home, working a dull job with no optimism for anything else. Without much parental guidance, she again turned to the high school principal—Alexander MacKimmie, a name she instantly recalled almost sixty years later—and wound up at Saint Mary's College, a sister school to Notre Dame, in South Bend, Indiana. However strange and even self-sabotaging a landing place this was for a half-Jewish girl who had hated Catholic school, where she went was less important than the fact that she was leaving home, breaking free of environmental constraints.

At Notre Dame, Michelle barely tolerated the religious instruction but loved the football tradition. Paul Hornung was the star football player and campus heartthrob. On game weekends, she participated in the traditional Friday march to the Grotto—the replica of the Grotto of Our Lady of Lourdes in France—with lighted candle. She worked year-round, in paying jobs that precluded volunteering at the student newspaper, to help her father with expenses, and she graduated in four years with a degree in English literature. She went home and added an education degree from the University of Connecticut. Almost five foot eight, brunette and pretty, she had no shortage of male suitors, but she married Joseph Musler, a high school classmate and fellow UConn student.

She had a son, Brandon, then two miscarriages. Her obstetrician told her that carrying another child to full term was unlikely. But she had a second son, Bruce, and in rapid succession three girls, Darcy, Devon, and Blair—five children born within a decade, four redheads and the dark-haired Bruce.

Friends would forever be amazed doing the math of her prolific reproductive powers. She couldn't explain the reasoning, much less the pace, ultimately guessing it was the Irish in her, and the need to create the dynamic family structure she had grown up without. The upshot, she said, was that "all the fantasies—journalism, everything—ended when I had five kids." Temporarily, anyway. But with the purchase of a home in the Three Lakes Park section of Stamford, Michelle settled into motherhood, a suburban lifestyle that had the superficial trappings of comfort but came with strings attached—ambitions shelved and gender stereotypes served. Her 1965 holiday letter, sent to family and friends in what would become an annual tradition, was laced with humor that betrayed her skepticism of her new lifestyle:

*Suburban living has to be experienced in order to be
believed. Since every wife functions primarily as a
chauffeur, it is mandatory for all female inhabitants of
Connecticut's Gold Coast to come equipped with a
steering wheel strapped to her chest. I am best identified
in my neighborhood as the '65 white Pontiac station
wagon (my close friends call me Catalina for short).*

Still, she enjoyed her busy existence as a parent and also
found time to take up jogging and yoga (before everyone and
their mother were doing it). In a conservative environment, she
wasn't shy about her liberal politics, despairing over the Vietnam War and the assassinations of Martin Luther King Jr. and
Robert Kennedy. But even her cynical version of suburban bliss
had term limits. Her husband was unfaithful and financially
unreliable. The marriage was all but over by her early thirties.

Out of financial need, she entered the workforce, teaching
English at a local high school, along with yoga. But the course of
her professional life changed when she accepted a paid intern-
ship during summer break in 1972 at the Stamford-based Xerox
Corporation, hoping to stay busy for the summer and to make
some extra money in the process. Her boss, an executive named
Derwin Fox, had a mandate to make the staff more gender
diverse—which in those days meant a woman or two. He saw potential in Michelle and corralled her at summer's end to offer her
an editorial slot in the development of audio-visual educational
programs for vocational high schools and colleges. He asked
what it would cost him for her to leave teaching, where Michelle
was earning roughly seven thousand dollars a year.

"Eight thousand?" she said.

"Dear, we can't afford to pay you that little."

They settled on low five figures. A career portal opened and Michelle charged through. The job required long days and nationwide travel—not the easiest juggling act for a single mother of five. However hectic it was making sure her children were looked after while she was away, there was no turning back. Michelle was a career striver unleashed, as she wrote in her 1972 holiday letter:

> I am blissfully happy in my work. Needless to say, I see a lot less of my children but I'm a helluva lot nicer when I do. And when faced with the decision—what do they want more, mommy or money—they chose just as you would expect devoted offspring to choose: "Get the money, ma!"

Over the next six years, Michelle rose from her starter position to senior project manager and then to national account manager for Xerox's major accounts group. She dealt exclusively with Fortune 500 companies, mostly with successful, leveraged men. No longer just a stressed-out suburban mom, she devoted a small fortune to styling herself for success—jewelry, blazers, shoes, the works. As a woman navigating corporate America in the seventies and seeking respect from the men who surrounded her, she believed she had to project her authority.

At Xerox, a colleague happened to ask her to a Knicks-Celtics game during the 1973–74 season. The Knicks were defending NBA champions, the hottest sports show in town, though in the final year of keeping their storied lineup—Willis Reed, Walt Frazier, Dave DeBusschere, Bill Bradley, and Earl Monroe—intact.

From childhood on, Michelle had been a casual pro basketball fan, in large part because her brother had played and followed the sport and she had chased after him to the neighborhood courts. She had taken in the occasional Knicks game with her husband and young sons. Her favorite player was the acrobatic Elgin Baylor of the Los Angeles Lakers, but it was difficult to live in the New York metropolitan area during the late sixties and early seventies without falling under the Knicks' championship spell. Rooting for Reed, Frazier, and friends also made for more partisan holiday arguments with her brother, who had remained in central Connecticut, a Boston Celtics fan.

As her professional status grew, Michelle suddenly had access to company tickets. She went to another game, and another, and eventually splurged on her own ticket package. Her seats weren't anywhere near courtside, but with every renewal came an upgrade, Michelle edging closer to the action. She finally made it there by decade's end, with a direct cross-court view of the home-team bench. In 1983, the Knicks came over to her side, moving their bench directly in front of her. It meant a partially obstructed view of the game, but the unmatched sideline exposure to the players was worth it.

She loved everything about this new playground, including its social possibilities. Befriending her courtside neighbors, Michelle began making the pre- and postgame scenes in Charley O's, the popular bar-restaurant establishment on the Thirty-third Street side of the building. She was ubiquitous and happy to talk to pretty much anyone. She made new, unlikely friends.

"You'd see her all the time—behind the bench, in the bar, at parties," said Harry Robinson, the statistician on the Knicks' radio broadcasts, another Garden lifer and Charley O's regular.

What Michelle learned fast was that she didn't need direct social access to the athletes in order to make their acquaintance and infiltrate their world. All that was required was getting to know a few people in their orbit. A Harry Robinson. A Cal Ramsey. She could—and did—become part of an entourage that ran with Reed, who retired after the 1973–74 season and basked in his celebrity about town until he began a brief run as the Knicks coach in 1977.

Butch Beard, a late-career Knicks point guard who transitioned into assistant coaching and, later, broadcasting, was also part of that group. One time, he went to an early eighties party at a North Jersey home that Ray Williams, a young Knicks guard, had purchased after securing a new contract. Beard walked in and spotted Michelle on the couch, in conversation with her puerile host from the mean streets of Mount Vernon, New York. Beard told himself, *I got to know what this is about.* He edged closer to hear Michelle lecturing Williams on how to be careful with his money. "I knew it was going in one motherfucking ear and right out the other," Beard said. "But I also thought, *OK, this is very cool on her part.*"

The more Michelle ventured to the Garden and elsewhere in her expanding basketball circle, the more she wanted to be there, all the while resigned to her family obligations that prevented an actual move into the city. But over the span of her six years at Xerox, her life changed dramatically. Though she was far from rich, the money faucet turned back on, which gave her some measure of security. She was forever grateful to Derwin Fox, who had unlocked this new world for her. Years later, she attended his funeral, a stranger to the assembled mourners. "He gave me a chance when women didn't get many," she stood up to tell them. "He saved my life."

In 1978, Michelle moved on from Xerox to PepsiCo in nearby Westchester County, developing management programs for human resources. In another job that required extensive travel, she arranged a deal for her one major perk: She could schedule her trips to ensure her attendance at Knicks home games.

She stayed at PepsiCo for three years, and leaped at the opportunity to work in Manhattan for Warner Amex. When she arrived, her former boss at PepsiCo wrote her a letter, an acerbic but complimentary bullet-point list of personal observations. "I don't miss you as much as I miss your AURA," he wrote. "Anyone who drives a secretary to tears just with one look has got to be a powerful person." Michelle tucked the letter into a home file, saving it as evidence of her corporate ascension, if not of her workplace compassion. She claimed she was never *that hard* on her support staff, just proud of the respect she commanded and received from her colleagues.

At Warner, where she eventually became a vice president of human resources operations, she impressed visitors to her office with a wall filled with photos of NBA stars and enlightened them in management classes she led by citing various coaches and players as examples of successful or failed leadership. She oversaw headquarters staff and field locations for Warner, a company of six thousand employees. She counseled and strategized with senior staff, designed performance-appraisal systems, and evaluated the performance of individual executives and the organization at large.

She stayed at Warner for five years, surviving a series of downsizing periods in which she became a real-life version of George Clooney's character from *Up in the Air*, an executive tasked with breaking the bad news to those laid off. Before the ax could fall on her, Michelle left for Chase Manhattan Bank, only to learn weeks later that her new company was also about to shed hundreds of employees. She eventually decided she had enough experience and relationships to strike out on her own, launching her global executive-training business, the Training Advantage Ltd., in 1986. Chase Manhattan helped her take the plunge by becoming her first client. Others soon signed on.

Unsurprisingly, running her own company proved more demanding than any of her previous jobs. Many workdays began at six a.m. and ended at midnight. Her travel schedule made a sportswriter's seem tame—one year, 1991, she had so much business that she logged eighteen trips to Cincinnati, five to Nashville, four to Seattle, three to Chicago, two to Hong Kong, and two to Thailand and Australia, among others that consumed fewer miles.

She still somehow managed to schedule her work life—and social life—around the Knicks. By the eighties, she kept like-minded company at the Garden, working women whose lives resembled hers more than any she had known in the suburbs. During her years at Warner Amex, working for the first time in Manhattan, Michelle had connected with Ernestine Miller, a single mother and a former high school and college athlete who had joined a different division of Warner not long after Michelle was hired. When men at the company learned of Miller's interest in sports, they would say, *Have you met Michelle?* Miller would become part of a rotation of three women sharing Michelle's second courtside seat—all single or divorced, all career professionals.

By this time, her children having reached young adulthood or in college, Michelle's business was thriving to the point where she could afford to rent an apartment in the city for the workweek—beginning with bland Midtown towers and, later, in Greenwich Village. There, with a view of Washington Square Park and sharing the neighborhood with NYU students, professors, street musicians, drug dealers, prostitutes, and undercover cops, she felt "alive, stimulated." Pushing fifty, she was an older version of Mary Tyler Moore, transitioned from the suburban stereotype of Laura Petrie to the professionally ambitious Mary Richards.

Being in the city meant a short subway ride to the Garden and a faster commute across the Hudson to the Nets' arena in New Jersey. (For a few years in the early to mid-eighties, Michelle also held season tickets for the Nets at the comparatively dowdy New Jersey Meadowlands arena. On game days, she would hitch a ride through the Lincoln Tunnel with Dave Sims of the *Daily News* or Nets executive Lewis Schaffel.) It reached the point to where she was attending four or five NBA games a week. But the Nets games merely represented another chance to catch that period's transcendent NBA megastars—Julius Erving, Magic Johnson, and Larry Bird—who never seemed to land on one of the local teams. The Garden was her special place, her chosen crowd, her stake in the Midtown heart of New York. She knew it from the moment she settled into her first courtside seat.

She told herself: *I'm home; this is it, where I want to be.*

....

In her 1980 Christmas letter, Michelle made a grand announcement, though sheepishly. She was going to Cleveland for a brief February vacation break. "Do I hear snickers? Did I hear someone comment that she's suicidal?" she wrote. Then she explained the underlying reason: She would be attending the 1981 NBA All-Star Game. She knew that some family members and old friends were bewildered by her growing basketball obsession. She also didn't care what they thought.

My earliest recollection of Michelle is from that All-Star weekend, when she crashed an evening gathering of media regulars at a downtown hotel with a filched *New York Times* press credential. Incongruous as that may sound, it was also somewhat par for the NBA course. All-Star weekend in those days was far from the orgy of corporate sponsorship revelers it would become in David Stern's expansionist reign, the genesis of which was still three years away. Anyone who knew anyone could pretty much talk their way into anything. Michelle was an artful and articulate enough schmoozer to take full advantage.

I don't remember what our conversation was about—the state of the Knicks would be a pretty good guess. I do remember walking away thinking, *Cool lady*. But when we reminisced in later years about how our friendship began, she always had a different version. She recalled earlier conversations at courtside before Knicks home games, prior to the 1981 All-Star weekend in Cleveland. And then one embarrassing evening outside the Garden when she was with one of her children and saw me heading in their direction.

"I said, 'Oh, that's Harvey, he covers the team. I *know* him.'"

And...?

"You walked right by without even acknowledging me," she said.

Completely possible, I knew, recalling how I was, at the time, living in my little bubble of ambition, unwaveringly focused on that day's pursuit of the almighty scoop. Michelle had many times teased me about the snub, but it came up again over dinner one night in Stamford, a couple of weeks after I had chauffeured her to the Knicks-Nets game at the outset of the 2017–18 season.

By this point, it was clear that I was going to be a frequent visitor on game nights, determined not to let Michelle transition from courtside to couch all on her own. The routine was set: a late-afternoon drive from Montclair, New Jersey, to beat rush-hour traffic, dinner at a nearby restaurant, and back to her place for the opening tip.

Michelle's condo was on Forest Street in an area dominated by high-rise buildings, within walking distance of a bustling commercial strip that included a small indie movie theater. Access to the theater and the nearby restaurants were prime considerations to buying the three-level condo as an empty nester, much to the consternation of her friends and family. All the home's stairs should have been a red flag for anyone already eligible for Medicare. Worse, Michelle's bedroom was on the top floor, directly above a room with workout equipment and walls filled with basketball *stuff*, the most prominent of which was a framed No. 1 Knicks jersey with "Musler" stitched onto the back.

She dismissed the stairs, even as navigating them became a challenge. "I go slow," she said. "It's fine." Except Michelle obviously wasn't fine and she couldn't hide it anymore. Through the previous dozen or so years, I had lost count of her surgeries and treatments—back, foot, hip, knee. She could list seven, while conceding she might have forgotten one or two. She'd also survived breast cancer, and sometime past her seventieth birthday she developed a neurological disorder with some Parkinson's-like symptoms, most visibly a tremor in the hands. The condition was treatable with medication—which Michelle refused to take, claiming it dulled her mentally. That was a nonstarter.

She endured the shaking in the way she did an ongoing and severe case of shingles, which aggressively attacked her eyes and head. She took to wearing one of the visors she ritually purchased every summer at the US Open—tennis being her second-favorite sport. Yanking the brim up and down helped stifle a maddening itch; she scratched and coped. Vulnerability had long been her sworn enemy. Even visits in rehab after surgery were practically forbidden, in large part because Michelle, clinging to the residual vanity of her old corporate life, hated being seen in any state of disrepair—and especially without her makeup.

"Can I come by?" I would ask.

"Absolutely not," she would say, telling me she would see me at the Garden as soon as she could get back there.

Being independent was the doctrine she lived by. In all the years I had known Michelle, only when her youngest child, Blair, was battling a rare form of cancer in Southern California around the turn of the century could she admit to a state of high anxiety—an anger at the terrible unfairness of it all, a terror that accompanied every ring of the phone.

None of her own surgeries were worth "bitching and moaning"

about. They were all problems that were, with any luck, fixable. But her latest medical challenge was entirely different, an unresolved mystery. The ministrokes—or transient ischemic attacks (TIAs)—had begun late in 2016, producing dizziness and numbness on her left side and requiring several brief hospitalizations for observation and medication, without much luck in determining the cause. Typical of Michelle, she told no one, not me or even her children, of her hospital stays—"What's the point of worrying them?" she'd tell me—until she was home, after the fact.

One rare exception was made when she'd had to break a Knicks game date with Wynn Plaut during the 2016–17 season. She felt the onset of a seizure in the late afternoon and called for help. With an ambulance idling out front, she hastily phoned Plaut to tell him she couldn't make the game. She would leave the tickets in a ziplock bag inside her mailbox.

"While you were about to go to the *hospital?*" I said.

"How else was he going to get the tickets?"

She dismissed any thought of making concessions—like not driving anymore—but admitted to worrying about her mental acuity. Her sardonic go-to line became: "I just want to wear a sign that says, 'I used to be smart.'" Maybe, I suggested, her perception of losing her edge was just typical aging stuff that she was overreacting to, adding for good measure that two days after seeing a film I often couldn't remember its name, the lead actors in it, or even what it was about. My optimism was patronizing, but the truth was that most of the time, Michelle still sounded to me—and other friends of hers I would consult—like herself. At dinner, as she settled with a glass of wine, her mind seemed sharp. On the phone, she asked, as always, about my wife, my sons, whatever work I was doing, things I had casually mentioned days or even weeks before.

Yet it was impossible to escape the ominousness of the seizures, especially after her neurologist raised the possibility that the ministrokes foretold a much bigger one, along with the creeping specter of dementia—a fate that to Michelle sounded truly worse than death. She likened it to "the movie with Julianne Moore," referring to Still Alice, a haunting tale of a middle-aged woman grappling with early-onset Alzheimer's. "That's what I think about, what I am terrified of," she said. "When I won't know what's going on." She paused, and with comic timing, added: "Please let me get hit by a bus before then."

These moments of gallows humor were awkward, to say the least. I wanted to say something soothing, but the best I seemed capable of doing was to steer the subject elsewhere, with levity. "Who knows how long, if ever, before that happens—and I don't mean the bus," I said. "Besides, you have to know what's going on—who else is going to do the job of listening to me?"

"You know that I've loved that job," she said. "I always wanted to know what made you tick, and how you got to where you were."

Michelle knew well that our paths to Madison Square Garden, while entirely different, had at least been alike in their improbability.

Three
....

The Making of
a Reporter

A s the 1990s became the 2000s, I had already been writing about sports for multiple decades. While I realized that I had many people's dream job—including my own!—I was also growing tired of the repetition of covering the same athletes and giant sporting events year after year. At the *Times*, whose sports section increasingly considered the planet to be its playing field, I began to take more advantage of the opportunities to travel far and wide—to Zimbabwe in Africa for a 2000 Davis Cup tennis competition; to the former Soviet Union two years later to report on a little-known NBA draft pick from Tbilisi in the Republic of Georgia; to Olympics across Europe and Asia.

But the offbeat story didn't necessarily require a marathon flight and a stamped passport. My interest in women's college basketball, for instance, grew out of my disdain for what the men's game had become: an exploitative meat market that left too many young men unpaid and uneducated. The women's game was different: Its star players typically stayed four years, long enough to graduate. The longer college career also created a more compelling narrative to chronicle.

At the 2005 Women's Final Four in Indianapolis, I became acquainted with a player whom I took an immediate and special interest in. Nicky Anosike, Tennessee's freshman center, happened to be from Staten Island, the borough of New York where I'd grown up. I located her in the locker room—not that difficult, at six feet four—and casually asked what neighborhood of the island she was from.

"West Brighton," she said.

Really, what street?

"Castleton Avenue."

Now I was *really* intrigued. What number, I asked?

She shot me a quizzical look but played along: "Ten seventy-seven."

"Wow," I said, "that's the same building that I lived in."

Apartment 2B—exactly one level above hers, it turned out, more than a quarter century apart.

The look on Anosike's face did not hide her skepticism: *This guy with graying hair and bookish glasses from the* New York Times *grew up in the projects?*

Granted, times had changed. The West Brighton I had grown up in was modest working class, but not impoverished. It was racially diverse, not predominantly black. It was sketchy but not yet ravaged by the scourge of drugs, guns, and gangs. But I sounded more authentic to Anosike when I told her that I had spent much of my childhood hanging around the development's outdoor basketball courts and correctly recalled the street name—Henderson

Avenue—along the perimeter. It turned out that we knew a small handful of the same neighborhood lifers spanning generations. Street cred apparently established, I learned more about Anosike: She was the sixth of eight children crammed into three bedrooms, while her Nigerian immigrant mother made certain everyone was fed and studied to earn a nursing degree at age forty. When Pat Summitt had recruited Anosike, the teenager had requested that the Tennessee coaching legend meet her and her family at her high school, not at home.

I didn't have to ask why. A city-subsidized cluster of eight-story buildings casting an unwelcome shadow over a gritty pocket on Staten Island's north shore, the West Brighton Houses were a place from which you wished to escape, not necessarily where you'd invite the person you hoped would help you get out.

Growing up in the projects could be a source of survivalist pride, provided you did get out. They were a place where a child could count on having playmates but a teenager could feel a sense of isolation—or alienation—from the outside world. To those of us on the inside, those who lived in modest homes on the surrounding streets seemed better off, if not well off. And those who *were* comparatively affluent didn't hide their sneers and snickers when the school bus pulled up to the projects to let us off.

My father, Gilbert, a Manhattan postal worker, worked hard against the odds to keep our family solvent, but credit card debt invariably mounted as he and my mother, Marilyn, fed and clothed three children, subsidized rent notwithstanding. The subliminal message when my mother would send me across the street for groceries with a shopping list and a request to put the charge on our tab was that we didn't have the cash to pay. Relying on the kindness of strangers, our meals could not be taken for granted.

The morning after interviewing Anosike, a few hours before the deadline of my Sunday column, I woke up thinking about a man named Mel Selznick, who had run the youth basketball leagues at the Staten Island Jewish Community Center a few miles from the projects. My family couldn't afford a membership—or at least keep up the monthly payments—but I had desperately wanted to play in an organized league. Carrying my gym bag, I would push open the side door into the building's cramped gymnasium, ready to make eye contact with Selznick. Never once did he fail to point me in the direction of the locker room, whether my dues were paid up or not. *Get dressed. Go play.* I was on unofficial scholarship.

My Sunday column told the story of how Summitt had recruited Anosike from the West Brighton Houses. But it was also about how Selznick—who had died suddenly that very week, just as plans had been finalized for a large reunion with him as the guest of honor—had helped rescue me.

I never dreamed of being a sportswriter—or any kind of writer, for that matter. I did love watching and reading about sports, usually in the solitude of my bedroom, locked away from the ongoing tensions caused by my family's financial travails and the inevitable pressures that piled up on my father, leading to the occasional outburst of anger.

He didn't care much about sports, but he did help ignite my

interest when he took me with him to a neighbor's apartment to watch Game 7 of the 1960 World Series with several men from our building. I was eight and largely clueless about baseball. But as the drama built in what ESPN would in 2010 call "the greatest game ever played," and the beer-fueled hysteria grew in that cramped living room as the Yankees and Pirates battled 9–9 into the home ninth inning, the first signs of my eventual addiction to sports surfaced: I cried and carried on so much after Bill Mazeroski homered for the Pirates to end the series that my father dragged me upstairs and sent me to my room.

A few years later, still seeking refuge from ongoing family drama, I began making regular visits to a quiet public library a few blocks from home to do schoolwork. There I discovered and devoured a series of novels by Duane Decker on a fictional baseball team called the Blue Sox. Reading about real sports was also good escapism. As a teenager and rabid sports fan, I grabbed the *New York Post* sports section from the back pocket of my father when he arrived home late afternoons after a long commute from the historic James A. Farley post office in Midtown Manhattan—a landmark building that sat directly opposite, of all places, Madison Square Garden.

By early high school, my older sister, Sharon, had gifted me a subscription to *Sports Illustrated*, which arrived every Thursday chock-full of the most sophisticated sportswriting America had to offer. But I can't say that any of those words infused me with an aspiration to be a sports journalist. I never wrote a word for my high school newspaper. I didn't fill notebooks with commentary about my beloved Yankees and Knicks.

In the projects, there weren't many—if any—professional role models. My father dropped out of high school to join the army, served in World War II, and braved the shelling of London as a firefighter. No one in multiple generations of my immediate or extended family had stepped foot in a college classroom.

I was the middle child between two girls, set in my late-1960s habits of listening to the emerging rock and folk music, smoking pot, playing hoops. I did my homework and had my share of complimentary teachers and academic triumphs. I still never gave much thought to what would come after high school—even after being chosen for a program targeting at-risk kids whose standardized test scores showed more promise than their grades.

By my senior year at Port Richmond High, a diverse public school in the shadow of the Bayonne Bridge on the island's north shore, many of my friends from outside the projects and especially the Jewish Community Center were touring colleges in upstate New York and beyond. My "tours" consisted of filling out an application for the City University system that was handed to me one day in class, listing three choices. Having had good fortune in the draft lottery, I had little chance of winding up in Vietnam; an older cousin had not been so lucky. Not because I had any good idea about a career path, but more because I couldn't think of anything better to do, I signed on to study at Brooklyn College, qualifying for free tuition.

But soon after high school graduation, before I even stepped into a college classroom, I received an offer that rerouted my life. At the JCC, I had become friendly with a volunteer coach, Danny Colvin, who was working his way into teaching while moonlighting on the sports desk of our local daily, the *Staten Island Advance*. All these years later, it remains unclear to me—and to

Colvin—why he asked if I was interested in doing menial work at the newspaper. The job required a drive into Manhattan late Saturday afternoons to the Associated Press building at Rockefeller Center in the ancient time not only before the internet but before transmission of glossy photos. After returning to the *Advance* newsroom, photos in hand, I would stay on until midnight to strip wires and attach the old tickertapes to the corresponding hard copy of the stories the editor was planning to run in the paper. Not the most glamorous work, but I certainly wasn't complaining: My previous jobs had been delivering newspapers and working the snack bar in the rear of a department store.

My time in college—which I lurched through, transferring from one school to another, leaking credits, managing to take an interest in a course here and there—hardly signaled an auspicious future. Nor did my newspaper career begin with great promise. I nearly blew it when it was barely underway. On a Saturday night in September 1972, the six p.m. first-edition deadline approached. Tom Valledolmo, the Sunday sports editor, told me to stay put in the narrow wire room to wait for the pending result on the Olympic gold-medal basketball game between the United States and the Soviet Union, in Munich, Germany. Any grudge match between the world's superpowers in the midst of a cold war was a major story. Waiting anxiously for the Associated Press report, I experienced that dreaded deadline pressure—the enemy against which I was destined to wage a career-long war— for the first time. Finally, the result hit the wire: USA 50, USSR 49, the piece's lede telling of two free throws by Doug Collins clinching the victory with three seconds remaining. I grabbed the hard copy, spooled the tape, attached it with a paper clip, and rushed from the room.

"We won . . . we won!" I announced, holding up the goods, forgoing journalistic neutrality I didn't yet comprehend.

"Get it out right away," Valledolmo said, pointing toward the composing room.

With that story set, the early edition was done. I returned to my desk, the deadline adrenaline rush subsiding, proud of my effort, ready for a break between editions. I don't know what compelled me to go back into that wire room about twenty minutes later. At that hour on any Saturday in September, the sports wire clattered away nonstop, full of baseball and college football results. Left unattended for even a short while, the paper would back up, bunched to the floor. More out of curiosity than presumed need, I perused the stories, one after another, until I reached the one that nearly stopped my heart. It was a resend of the basketball result.

ALERT: USSR 51, USA 50.

The new lede told the tale of the disputed replay of the final three seconds that became an excruciating part of American sports lore. I burst out of the wire room with the tape and paper, yelling, "They replayed it . . . they replayed it!" Valledolmo had no clue what I was talking about. When I explained what had happened, he turned pale, bolted from his seat, grabbed the tape from me, and raced out to the composing room. The first-edition run, already begun, ground to a halt.

Lord knows whatever happened to the handful of Sunday *Advances* that had the Americans winning the gold. All I know is that Valledolmo, bless him, didn't blame or fire me. In fact, shortly after my graduation from a division of New York's City University system in 1975, he gave me my first full-time job as the newly minted sports editor. As a full-time staffer, I covered high school and local college games, manned the phones, and learned old-school page layout and photo cropping. At a local paper that required everyone to chip in as needed, I covered school board meetings and wrote obituaries for the news desk. I worked closely with Valledolmo, who later became a night sports editor at the *Post*, and with Jay Price, a superb columnist who would have been a star at any of the city's major dailies had he chosen that route. The *Advance* was my Columbia School of Journalism.

A perk I earned by the midseventies was covering Saturday night Knicks games at the Garden, filing deadline stories and squeezing into the locker-room scrum of famous New York scribes for interviews with the remaining legends of the championship teams, Walt Frazier and Earl Monroe. Each week, as I watched the players warm up from my seat at the very end of the press table, as much a fan as I was a reporter, the same Knicks PR employee would wander my way and ask, "And you are . . . ?"

"Staten Island," I would say.

The *Advance* was an excellent local newspaper, covering the city's most rural borough across the Narrows, though rare was the New Yorker from the four other boroughs who knew it existed. Didn't matter to me. I was a full-time working sports journalist. I suddenly had direction and a career in the making, and I grew more determined, every time I ventured to the Garden, to make that Knicks employee remember my name. That opportunity would come sooner than I could have hoped for.

. . . .

The *Post* had long been my sports section of choice, a collection of creative writers whose prose was enhanced by the generous overnight deadlines of journalism's endangered species, the afternoon newspaper. Larry Merchant. Paul Zimmerman. Vic Ziegel. Henry Hecht. Maury Allen. The young Mike Lupica and Larry Brooks. I read them faithfully throughout my *Advance* years, and tried on occasion a little too transparently to imitate them.

Much to the chagrin of a parochial readership expecting a straightforward names-and-numbers account of a high school game, I was intent on churning out innovative gems, a few of which went woefully wrong—like my infamous "I Am a PSAL Baseball" story, in which I assumed the identity of a ball being "spanked" into submission by a hot-hitting high school team. Letters and calls flooded the sports department from coaches and parents. Beyond bewilderment, some readers went so far as to ask: *Was your reporter drunk, or high?*

I loved my years at the *Advance*, where our staff basketball team played school faculties all over the island, entertaining gyms full of students while trying not to make fools of ourselves. But the *Post* remained my dream job, and the call that came on a spring day in 1977 left me joyous, if a bit dazed. It was Phil Mushnick, a JCC friend, wondering if I'd be interested in leaving my reporting position in a small pond for a night sports clerking role in the big one. Mushnick had joined the *Post* as a copyboy after college, graduated to clerking, and was now apprenticing as a reporter, covering professional soccer, the New York Cosmos of Pelé and Beckenbauer.

I went to the paper's headquarters on South Street in Lower Manhattan, facing the East River and the landmark Brooklyn Bridge, to see the sports editor. Mushnick had warned me: Jerry Lisker was more Runyonesque character than ink-stained wretch. I wore a suit, neatly brushed my longish brown hair, carried my résumé and clips. Without looking up from his desk, Lisker barked, "You know sports?"

"Yes," I said.

"Can you type?"

"Yes," I said, omitting that my skills were limited to my index fingers.

"Come in tonight at eight," he said.

I arrived a few minutes early to an empty office, until a gangly young guy with dark flowing hair, Jackson Browne cut, ambled in.

"You Araton?" he said.

"Yeah," I replied.

"Bob Drury," he said, offering a hand. "I was hired today by Jerry Lisker. He told me to ask for you."

I guessed I was not only hired, but already in charge.

Within a year, Drury was the beat reporter for the NFL's Giants and I was covering the Knicks. Such was the fast-changing state of affairs at a newspaper founded in 1801 by Alexander Hamilton and published for decades by the passionately liberal Dorothy Schiff until 1976. She cashed out and let her beloved progressive baby, which had crusaded against the likes of Joe McCarthy and European fascism before its many competitors, fall into the sensational, right-wing clutches of Rupert Murdoch.

Veteran reporters were largely resistant to the Murdoch way, adding "the *Post* has learned" to any negligible news exclusively obtained and "told the *Post*" to the most innocuous of quotes. Their young replacements, myself included, were less dedicated to traditional norms of journalistic circumspection, even when the results were difficult to stomach.

In my earliest days on the Knicks beat I was promoted to in 1978, I wrote about Willis Reed's plaintive cry for clarity on his head-coaching position. When I asked him if he was worried about circulating rumors that Sonny Werblin, the Madison Square Garden president, wanted to replace him, Reed said that his youthful team was naturally affected by such instability. The players needed to know if he was "in or out."

We were in Seattle at the time, three hours behind New York, too late to call the Garden for a response from Werblin. The next day, my carefully constructed lede was dismissively rewritten to fit a screaming back-page headline: IN OR OUT. As soon as I heard about it, I called Werblin to explain that Reed's quote was actually expressed as more of a plea. He thanked me for the clarification, but fired Reed a few days later, telling people inside the organization that nobody was going to give him an ultimatum. My editors were naturally thrilled about my tabloid baptism in what amounted to a trial run on the beat—helping to get Reed, one of my basketball heroes, fired.

Every day at the *Post* pretty much began with an exhortation from the desk—"Write for the back page"—reverberating in my brain. That was meant as pressure to report something newsy, splashy, that would grab readers by the collar as soon as they flipped the paper over, front to back. We all worked with the daily terror of being beaten by our competitors—to the point where some nights I would drive from my apartment in Staten Island to a newsstand in Midtown for copies of the night editions of the *Times* and *Daily News*.

I slept better knowing there would be no morning surprise.

Even more ominous was the searing scrutiny of the *Post*'s own Peter Vecsey, the city's most renowned basketball columnist, a beat watchdog and self-appointed critic of competing basketball reporters, including his own colleagues. Journalists and especially young journalists lead anxious lives, imagining themselves a blown story or two from career extinction. At Murdoch's blood-and-guts tabloid, that pressure was amplified and infused into our daily regimen: back page or bust.

I was as insecure as the next guy, perhaps more so. I hadn't come from a family of journalists, or professional strivers, people who had experienced and understood the burden of a competitive work environment. In retrospect, I don't know which I needed more during those early *Post* years: a friend to keep me grounded, an adviser to keep me directed, or a well-placed source to help keep me enlightened—and employed.

When I met Michelle, I lucked into all three.

Four

Courtship

If there is one time-honored truth in sports journalism—or journalism of any kind, really—it's that nobody wants to talk to a nobody. Such was my predicament when Greg Gallo, my editor at the *Post*, walked over to my desk one summer morning in 1979 and told me to "get Steinbrenner on the phone."

At the time, I had virtually no name recognition outside Madison Square Garden. And far more than any basketball player, George Steinbrenner was the most sought-after sports figure in New York, while his two-time defending champion Yankees were the city's hottest story—in no small part because Steinbrenner was a walking, talking back-page headline. On this day, word got around that his general manager, Al Rosen, was leaving the organization, which meant either that he'd been fired or that he couldn't take another day of being screamed at by the volcanic owner. On summer hiatus from my new Knicks beat responsibilities, I was working the day rewrite desk—cobbling together breaking news for the afternoon editions and, on occasion, covering for another beat reporter who was traveling or unreachable in the days long before cell phones.

Get Steinbrenner on the phone. Sure, right away, no problem. I dialed the office he mainly worked out of in Tampa, Florida, and was predictably stonewalled by his secretary, who had me on hold for minutes while Steinbrenner no doubt waved her out of the office at the mention of a name he'd never heard. What to do, except admit failure? Far from secure on my beat and at the paper, I stalled for a while, keeping the phone in my ear, before being inspired by a wave of desperation. I dialed Steinbrenner's office again and spoke quickly, authoritatively.

I told the secretary, "This is Mickey—I need George."

"Hold on, Mick, I'll get him."

Mickey Morabito was the Yankees' lead PR guy, a job description that was shorthand for Steinbrenner's 24-7 personal press secretary and repository for letting off steam. Within seconds, Steinbrenner was on the line and I was hemming and hawing my way through an apologetic explanation of who I really was and why I had called. Inclined to slam down the phone, he couldn't help but give me a lecture—only to come around to the conclusion that he admired my audacity.

"Don't ever do this again—but what do you need?"

I got my quote—a rather bland one for the bombastic boss, but I had done as I was told: I'd *gotten* Steinbrenner. The lesson was clear: Pathways to success didn't come easy to a new kid on the beat. I had to make the most of any opportunity I had. And at the Garden, a rather obvious one was Michelle.

As charming as she was during our earliest conversations,

my initial interest in her had much to do with the understanding that she was something of a Knicks insider, a potential source. When the Knicks relocated their bench directly in front of her, she even had a direct line to the team huddle. Whatever was going on there, I, as the *Post*'s beat reporter, the emergent Murdoch-subsidized muckraker, figured that she was likely to be privy to it. She had to know which players were ticked off when removed from a game. Who had cursed out a teammate or two during a time-out. The poor souls in the crosshairs of the coaches, especially after the congenitally profane Hubie Brown had replaced Red Holzman the previous season and begun his reign of coaching terror. The early stages of our friendship thus were less a recognition of like-mindedness and more a process born of self-interest. Stopping by Michelle's seat before every game was strategic, even if I didn't have her undivided attention. I certainly had no arrangement of exclusivity; in fact, I had plenty of company.

My enduring image of Michelle at courtside is with her tote bag of daily newspapers at her feet; a stream of pregame or half-time visitors wedged into the narrow area between her seat and the aisle behind the Knicks bench; and a security guard making a half-hearted attempt to keep traffic moving, but ultimately deferring to her and putting up with the logjam. They came from all walks of Garden life—employees; fellow fans; and players' wives, girlfriends, and mothers, varying from game to game, season to season; while neighboring fans watched in bewilderment. Bob Berne, a real estate developer who for decades sat behind Michelle and whose wife, Steffi, initially mistook her for some high-powered Garden executive, summed up the scene perfectly when he once asked her, "Do you come here to watch the game or to take attendance?"

But the most welcome visitors were the sportswriters. Her appreciation and envy of our backstage access was most obvious to the women who sat beside her and could see how important we were to Michelle. They seldom imposed on the conversations. "It was her time to shine, to be on the inside," said Drucie De Vries, whom Michelle had met when De Vries married a Greenwich-based businessman who was a friend of Michelle's. She lived in Greenwich until the marriage dissolved; she then moved to Manhattan and, like Michelle, rebooted her social life at courtside with the Knicks.

De Vries was amazed by how Michelle seemed to have a rapport with virtually everyone on press row. Even an esteemed columnist like George Vecsey of the *Times*—Peter's older brother, who dropped by the Garden mostly for the highest-profile games—would make it his business to stroll over for a pregame chat about the latest political news, the weather, and, of course, the state of the Knicks. As Vecsey remembers it, Michelle was "like a queen sitting there, but with the eyes and ears of a trained spy."

Indeed, she was always watching closely, more than any of us really knew at the time. Because Michelle, not unlike me, also had an agenda rooted in the fulfillment, at least abstractly, of her own adolescent sports journalist's ambition. "Your job is my fantasy job," she would tell me years later. "I lived vicariously through you because I wanted to *be* you."

The way reporters always kept an eye on one another in the locker room, paranoid about whom their counterparts at competing papers were talking to, so it was, in a sense, with Michelle. On any given night, my main competitors during those early days on the beat—especially Dave Sims of the *Daily News* and Roy Johnson of the *Times*—might have beaten me to her side pregame. None of us had a clue as to why this fortysomething woman from the far northern suburbs was so fascinated by what we did, nor did we bother to ask. If she had pertinent information, we were all ears. Whatever friendships developed began with that simple truth.

So how did I gain the inside edge with Michelle? How did she become *my* courtside coconspirator? It helped that Sims exited the newspaper business in the early eighties to work in broadcasting and Johnson left the *Times* and New York for a job in Atlanta. But what drew me closer to her more than any other factor was the pure luck of toiling for the *afternoon* newspaper. The *Post* would eventually launch a morning edition and later completely abandon the dying p.m. market. But my tactical advantage as a young beat reporter was that I had all night—or at least until the early morning hours—to file my stories.

Unlike reporters for the morning dailies, I could spend as much time as I needed in postgame locker rooms, sidling up to players while my competitors rushed upstairs to sweat out their deadlines. My notebook full, I would work my way down to the bar, where I could find Michelle, my new friend and Knicks pipeline, among the lingering players, their entourages, and assorted extras.

In the days before the internet and ESPN dominance, when newspapers were far and away the primary sources of sports team news, she waited to hear from me what had transpired in the locker room, a preview of what she would read in the next day's *Post*. Michelle especially loved the inside dope, the locker room chatter only reporters had access to. While George Vecsey was the sports columnist she most admired, Michelle—like most basketball junkies in the city—was also addicted to Peter's "Hoop du Jour" offerings in the *Post*. Nowhere in the country was there anyone quite like Peter Vecsey, the first of the full-time, sport-specific insiders now so prevalent across the sports-media landscape. His thrice-weekly columns were filled with league-wide secrets, grapevine scuttlebutt, and mordant asides. As a result, the *Post*'s sports section had the cachet of being the city's most basketball savvy.

While Michelle was a devoted reader of the *Times*, if there was one daily sports section that she absolutely had to read, it was the *Post*'s. "My dark secret," she called it, sheepish about the paper's unapologetic exploitation of scandal, crime, and ultraconservative politics.

I would provide her a run-down of what had occurred in the Knicks' locker room, and in return, Michelle would share with me what she had seen behind the bench and heard in the bar. She wasn't then or ever a basketball X's and O's strategist who could provide a dissertation on defensive rotations or the intricacies of the high screen and roll. But she *was* a professional observer of people and behavior, and the part she loved most about being so close to the bench was seeing how the coaches and players reacted to the drama and the pressure, for better or worse. While most fans used time-outs for grabbing a beer, gabbing with friends, or, in later years, checking their email and Twitter feeds, Michelle was locked into the goings-on in the Knicks' team huddle. And I—given the time to go beyond the straight details of the generic game story—wanted to get them into my stories. Our interests were aligned.

Some of what she would tell me was just gossip she knew I wouldn't use. Some of it was valuable as background material. But on occasion, Michelle's insider access actually led to a jackpot, a back-page *Post* exclusive. The first of these was set in motion by a phone call one summer day, with Michelle telling me that she had heard *something*: Ray Williams, the Knicks' talented young guard, was in talks to sign as a free agent with the Cleveland Cavaliers.

Where had she heard that, I asked, knowing it could have been from any number of people.

"Mederia," she said.

The wife of Marvin Webster, the Knicks' seven-foot center, Mederia Webster was a twentysomething woman far from her North Carolina home, with a young son and a need for a good friend. Or better yet, a maternal substitute.

If Mederia Webster was offering this tidbit, I knew it was more than a rumor. A quick call to Williams's agent, who was happy to get the word out to pressure the Knicks into stepping up with an offer, was all I needed to confirm the story. If I had suspected that Michelle might be my secret weapon on the Knicks beat, this scoop confirmed it.

There were more leads, more exclusives originating with Michelle, including one of the biggest Knicks stories of the early eighties. In late September 1982, she called me one morning and coyly told me she had heard from someone—this time, she wouldn't say whom—that the Knicks were about to reel in Bernard King, one of the league's rising stars, as a free agent.

I immediately called King's agent but got no response. Knowing information like this could spread quickly, I took a calculated risk and called John Hewig, the Knicks' public relations director. "I hear you guys are signing Bernard King," I said with feigned certainty.

Hewig laughed. "What took you so long?" he said, respecting the fact that I apparently had an informed source, but with no idea that that source was a well-placed season ticket holder. Hewig, who understood the beat-reporting game better than most PR people, honored my scoop and promised not to officially release the story until my back-page report was out in one of the *Post*'s afternoon editions.

Michelle was thrilled when I called to tell her that Hewig had confirmed the King signing and the story was being fast-tracked into the paper. It was almost as if *she* had broken the news. She still wouldn't divulge her source's identity; I never did find out. Like any credible journalist, she was suddenly protecting her people.

I was by then developing other Knicks sources, but there's no doubt that my friendship with Michelle helped me to establish a reputation on the beat, cement my job at the *Post*, and survive a period of my career that was fraught with insecurity.

She once told me that one of the main reasons she had befriended and helped me—beyond my eagerness to indulge her vicarious reporter's whimsy—was because she found me *interesting*. Angst-ridden, but interesting. She compared me to a Woody Allen character—too mired in self-analysis to fully appreciate my good fortune and allow for the possibility that talent and hard work had much to do with it and would sustain it. Dealing with guarded or emotionally repressed male executives in her corporate training work was frustrating, Michelle told me. I, on the other hand, seldom hid my inner conflict, but at the same time I was able to at least laugh at myself as a means of coping.

The best example of this, she always said, was a back-page essay I wrote for the *Daily News*'s Sunday magazine in the mid-eighties. In the piece, I recounted a farcical dream that I'd had in which I found myself in the semifinals of the US Open, along with Jimmy Connors, Bernard King, and Isaac Allen, an old basketball buddy from the West Brighton Houses.

In the dream, I was furious that I'd drawn Connors, an actual tennis great, as opposed to one of the two basketball players, and was arguing with a tournament official before the dream ended with me warming up with Connors on the big stadium court.

"Don't you see how positive that is?" Michelle said when I sheepishly described the dream. It obviously represented different stages of my life, she said. Basketball was the game I'd always been involved with. Tennis was practically a foreign concept to me—not exactly a sport whose reach extended to kids in the projects—until a long newspaper strike during the summer of 1978. Several makeshift dailies appeared to fill the news vacuum, and one hired me to cover the US Open, despite my knowing little about the sport. Connors demolished Bjorn Börg in the men's final in front of a raucous New York crowd. I immediately fell in love with the game and took up playing it soon after.

Tennis, Michelle insisted, was the part of the dream that represented my relatively new professional life that was so different from the work my family members had typically done. I was

understandably fearful of playing Connors because he symbol-
ized the uncertainty and insecurity of the challenge far outside
my family's comfort zone. But the dream had ended with me on
the court with Connors, meeting the challenge, overcoming my
fears. That all made sense. And so did the headline that my editor, Vic Ziegel, wrote: A BASKET CASE. Michelle laughed hysteri-
cally when she read it. She could admit that she had grappled
with her own impostor syndrome as she rose through the corporate ranks, wondering if her success might be fleeting—and not
necessarily deserved, given her family background.

Fair enough. It certainly was true that I hadn't grown up with
a belief that anything was possible, much less with any sense of
entitlement. My father's idea of a good job was the one that was
most likely to last. He was chronically averse to taking risks. If
you had what seemed to be a secure position, why in the world
take a chance on going elsewhere?

I can still hear him cautioning me—"What do you need it
for?"—before I jumped to the *Post* from the *Staten Island Advance*.
As much as that job offer and move was a fantasy come true, I
still struggled with leaving my friends, my routines, my secure
place. The prospect of change was even worse when the *Daily
News* recruited me to cover the Knicks in the fall of 1982. Even
with a raise in salary and the chance to write for a newspaper
with a larger circulation, I was torn with indecision about leaving the *Post*, where an army of young recruits made for a free-
wheeling work environment and an active social life. But as
much as Michelle preferred the *Post*'s sports section to the *Daily
News*'s, which focused more on football and baseball, she urged
me to move on—if for no other reason than to escape Peter

Vecsey's shadow. Plus, she argued, no one's career ever suffered because they were the object of a competitor's desire.

"You'll go there, make it better, and you'll stand out more," she said. Her powers of persuasion, no doubt what made her so good in her work, helped convince me to take the plunge. In retrospect, it also underscored how close a friend and how much of an influence she had become in so short a time, less than two years.

In that sense, I had Michelle to thank for an even greater fateful life change. The following summer, during the NBA off-season, my *Daily News* editor assigned me to cover the inaugural championship game of the USFL, an upstart spring football league that would ultimately suffer the self-sabotaging consequences of granting a franchise to an egomaniacal Manhattan real estate developer named Trump. I wasn't crazy about spending a midsummer week away and initially resisted the assignment. Steve Serby, my former *Post* colleague, talked me into going, convincing me it would be a big party, a Brand X Super Bowl. The game was in Denver, and there, checking into the league office in the ballroom of the downtown Marriott to get my credential, I met Beth Albert, a twenty-four-year-old publicist for the league and a mutual friend of a sports copy editor at the *Daily News*.

The championship game was memorable mostly for a reason unrelated to football. As time expired, police confronted fans rushing onto the field, setting off a melee. Watching this unfold on deadline, frantically trying to shoehorn the chaos into a game story, I looked at Beth incredulously as she blithely handed out printed player quotes from the locker rooms.

"Can you see that there's a damn riot going on?"

The following afternoon, after partying too hard and missing my morning flight home, I ran into Beth at the airport gate and stammered through an apology for my deadline rudeness. She laughed it off. The most serendipitous night of drinking and oversleeping led to a prolonged conversation, a dinner date, then another at a Yankees game. We were engaged by Thanksgiving.

When I had first met Michelle, I had been involved in a dysfunctional relationship that had weighed heavily on me, to the point where I was literally losing sleep. She wasted little time in advising me to extricate myself from it. But from the time I introduced her to Beth at a Knicks game, her instincts told her what I would soon come to believe: I had met the right woman.

Because Beth was from Greenwich and her parents lived two exits from Michelle on the Merritt Parkway, there was ample opportunity for the two women to get to know each other. Beth, Michelle agreed, was smart, beautiful, approachable ("I can see why she's in PR," she said), and ineffably high on life. In other words, the perfect personality complement to me, given my Woody Allen–esque tendency—as Michelle never tired of telling me—to see half-full glasses as almost empty.

"You hit the jackpot," she congratulated me, while adding a few choice words ("Grow the fuck up") when I worried about how Beth's family would regard the union of the son of a city postal worker and the Greenwich-bred daughter of a Yale-educated lawyer.

Yet she also sympathized with me when I grew to fear that we had rushed into an engagement and didn't really know each other well enough with the marriage date fast approaching.

Wedding plans had consumed my time with Beth when I wasn't on the road with the Knicks. We had never had an argument, much less a crisis. As a date of consequence approached—the printing of invitations—I confided to Michelle that I wasn't sure I was ready to get married and was considering a postponement. And who knew better than Michelle that rushing into marriage was not a good idea?

"If she's mature enough to be her own person, she'll understand," she said. But Beth was six years younger than I was, still very much under her parents' influence, and I worried that she might feel pressured by them to tell me it was now or never. "Then you'll have a very difficult decision to make, won't you?" Michelle said. "But from everything I know about Beth, I think you'll be pleasantly surprised."

She was right. When I broke the news, Beth took it tearfully but respectfully. In lieu of a wedding, we traveled together to Europe that summer. The pressure was off. It was just us, on the road, enjoying each other. I knew before the trip was over that we would soon reschedule the wedding. We were married in June 1985, the reception taking place under a tent on the front lawn of my new in-laws' home.

Michelle called me after receiving her invitation to say she was thrilled to receive one, but that she knew how difficult it could be to pare down guest lists—was there really room for someone I hadn't known that long? However long it had been, since that Cleveland All-Star game or sometime prior, I told her that she already was a special friend, on my A-list.

We sat Michelle at a table with several of my basketball sportswriting pals, all of whom she knew from being around the

Garden—a few who, like me, leaned and even cried on Michelle's shoulder from time to time. She was not quite one of the gang, though—more the equivalent of a trusted bartender, the good listener. But her own life—or at least past life—was more or less off-limits.

Over the decades, Michelle had shared her most personal details only with friends from outside the NBA world. At courtside, she was only Michelle Musler, high-powered executive and rabid Knicks fan. She had also become, over time, a fan advocate of sorts, appearing in numerous newspaper articles—including my own—as an increasingly price-gouged loyalist more frustrated by the Knicks' organizational upheaval and inability to win a championship. But in 2000, interviewed for a *New York Times* story on the psychology of sports fanaticism, she offered a glimpse into the genesis of her involvement with the Knicks.

"My ex-husband ran away with the lady next door and I didn't seem to fit into suburbia anymore," she said. "The Knicks gave me a purpose, something to do, a place to go. As a fan, I guess, there is a sense of belonging. That you are a part of something . . . What happened through the years is that the Knicks have become my social life."

She would, years later, tell me that she had regretted the quote, feeling embarrassed that she had revealed too much. She worried that she had stereotyped herself as a jilted, embittered woman desperately trying to fill time in an otherwise empty life.

But the mother of five was by then a grandmother of three. Her daughters had all moved west and south but Brandon, her firstborn, lived in Manhattan with a daughter, Dylan; her other son, Bruce, had two sons, Andrew and Sam, in a suburb of Boston. Michelle, meanwhile, was still thriving in her executive-training business. She had her inner Knicks circle—myself very much a part of it—her yoga classes, and a multitude of friends in Stamford and New York. She also held a seat on the board of the prestigious School of Visual Arts in Manhattan, the result of a spontaneous friendship she had struck up with Silas Rhodes, the school's founder, while sitting in an adjacent corporate box at the US Open.

Outwardly, at least, she had long moved past bitterness; her life was far from empty. But the Garden had always, by design, represented her refuge, her clean social slate. And because the story had appeared in the *Times*, the newspaper she assumed most of her friends at the Garden read, she felt exposed, vulnerable to pity—the very judgments she had sought to escape at courtside.

Divorces happen. They are not big news, anything to hide. The failure of Michelle's marriage, however, was anything but ordinary. She made it sound like a Shakespearean tragedy, suburban-style. Only once was I able to see through the cool veneer she maintained on the rare occasions she talked about it. It was in Boston, at Bruce's 1988 wedding reception, when her ex drove up in a luxury car with the woman he had left her for, his second wife. The composed, pragmatic Michelle suddenly vanished, replaced by a fuming, profane version. It was a side of her I had never seen, the inverse of her identity—Michelle in need of emotional support. The reception was on a boat in Boston Harbor. As the guests boarded, Beth and I sat with her as she seethed, cursing under her breath, seemingly fighting back tears. I imagined that we had been invited for the purpose of supporting her—the first time I recall that our roles in the friendship were reversed.

She and Joe Musler had been married for roughly a decade, but Michelle always maintained that the relationship had steadily disintegrated before its official end as the sixties gave way to the seventies. Even during comparatively stable times, her husband wasn't around much, she said, chasing business opportunities and other interests, returning for brief reconciliatory periods. In the marriage's latter stage, when she knew he was having an affair with a neighbor, tragedy struck: The other woman's husband died suddenly. Michelle and Joe divorced soon after. He and the widowed woman eventually married and left town. Of the four adults involved, Michelle was the one who'd had to deal with the public fallout of two fractured families, the ensuing gossip, the lingering mystery and questions that could not definitively be answered.

It took a few years before she shared these unpleasant details, and the hardship that followed, with me. It was over drinks in Charley O's after a game; I don't recall how or why it came up, only that she explained it all without emotion, matter-of-factly, as if it had been part of a past life and the person sitting across the table from me had been reincarnated. As her friend, I was saddened to hear what she'd had to endure. As a journalist, I was fascinated, intrigued. Knowing what she had done with her life in the ensuing years, empowering herself to a corporate perch, I blurted out, half-kidding, "Your life is a book!" She laughed, but I could tell that the wishful journalist in her was intrigued by the thought.

Unsure of how much she wanted me to probe, it took me a while before I could work up the nerve to ask more specific questions about what it was like to live in what sounded like the plot of a soap opera. "Wherever I went, I could feel people looking at me and thinking, *Poor woman*," she said. But she had little time to feel sorry for herself, because if it was one thing to raise five young children in a marriage going bad, it was quite another to do it alone.

"What am I supposed to do with these kids?" she recalled pleading with her husband as he descended the stairs for the last time, suitcase in hand, Michelle less frantic about the end of the marriage than she was about the specter of parenting solo. "How am I going to take care of them?"

"Whatever you do," he said, "it'll be better than what I can do."

When Michelle recounted this conversation, she was willing to give her ex credit for having been right about *something*: She *had* survived. But not without a painful, epic struggle. "Most days, I wanted to just lock myself in that bedroom and lay there all day," she said.

Nights were worse: one insomnia-fueled stare-down with the ceiling after another, with daylight bringing another round of dread, first and foremost with financial despair. All the while, she tried to keep up the appearance of holding it together, digging deep for humor in her 1970 holiday letter:

> *The Muslers are alive and well and still living in the Land of Oz. In contrast to the burgeoning population explosion, though, we've reduced our numbers by one. In addition to alimony, I've acquired the kids, the dogs, the*

cats, the house, the car, the bills, the overflowing septic
tank and the psychiatrist twice a week . . .

Just like that, at least for public consumption, Joe Musler was stricken from the script, though Michelle's predicament was much worse than she had let on. Her visits to the psychiatrist—Dr. Simon Goldfarb, "who kept me functioning"—were a major stretch for her shrunken budget. Her ex had worked in the business world but was guided, she said, by an entrepreneurial spirit that could produce—and exhaust—copious sums of money. In the most harrowing of times, before she could begin her career ascent, the alimony she desperately needed to keep her household afloat dried up. Even child support could be sporadic. She had to get by with whatever he sent, some help from her family, and what she earned teaching.

Given the size of her brood and the number of bills, it was never enough. Corners and coupons were cut. Her shopping list amounted to food rationing. Clothing for the kids tended to be hand-me-downs and castoffs. Finances became so dire that Michelle considered going on welfare. She researched the possibility of moving the family to Israel or Australia in hopes of receiving resettlement assistance.

Ultimately, she stayed, deciding that her children, innocent of their parents' dysfunction, needed stability, familiarity, their neighborhood routines. She reasoned that they at least were young enough to move on, to reap the benefits of a community's sympathy. But for Michelle, remaining in Stamford was like reliving her post-tuberculosis period in high school; she was the popular girl turned social orphan. Some friends abandoned her.

Even worse, others pitied her. Couples would insist on paying for her at the movies when she agreed to go along as a third wheel, or put on their sad faces when they bumped into her there on a night out by herself. She was struck, even haunted by moments of pure humiliation. Invited to a holiday gathering of what she later would call the "two-by-two people," she found herself in conversation with a neighbor's husband. Within seconds, she was brushed backward by the wife barging in between them. In short, she said, "I didn't fit there anymore."

That was the night she decided she wouldn't have to. She had already survived her working-class childhood, her family's dysfunction, the plague of tuberculosis. She was determined not to let herself wallow in self-pity, to be that "poor woman." She defiantly recommitted herself to raising her children in Stamford and to meeting the challenge of lifting them out of financial deprivation. It was, after all, the early seventies, the women's liberation movement well underway. Michelle staked out a place for herself in it right in her kitchen, so anyone who stepped into her house—and mainly her children—would know where she was coming from, and where she was going.

Her pronouncement of independence, framed on the wall, read: "Some mothers bake brownies. Our mother makes money."

Five
....

Christmas Cheer

S till early in a career that would primarily exist on the fringes
of the professional game, Ron Cavenall was in his first and
only season with the Hubie Brown–coached Knicks. His arrival
in New York—and the NBA, for that matter—during the 1984–85
season was serendipitous, and largely attributable to a desper-
ate team.

A seven-footer who had averaged five points and five re-
bounds in the college basketball minors, at Texas Southern
University, Cavenall was spotted by Rick Pitino, then a Brown
assistant, while working as a basketball counselor at Kutsher's
Sports Academy in Monticello, New York. He joined a Knicks
team ravaged by injuries to its big men and including the likes
of the immortal Eddie Lee Wilkins from Gardner-Webb and Ken
"the Animal" Bannister from Saint Augustine's College.

Cavenall spent most of his time at the end of the Knicks
bench—in other words, directly in front of Michelle, who wasn't

thrilled with the quality of play but whose journalistic-like curiosity was not dampened by the cast of marginal players in front of her. She loved hearing their backstories, and Cavenall's was uncommonly interesting. Ignored in the ten-round 1981 college draft, he had wound up on the Harlem Magicians, a barnstorming team formed in the image of basketball's clown princes, the world-famous Globetrotters, after befriending the daughter of the team's owner and star, Marques Haynes, in college. Haynes hired Cavenall for the Kutsher's summer job—he signed on as the tallest counselor in the Catskills, and the next thing he knew he was suiting up for the Knicks.

The son of a biology teacher, Cavenall had studied computer science and impressed Michelle with his realistic approach to his athletic career—he was already planning for its inevitable end with the assumption he wouldn't have much financial security to show for it. She, in turn, imparted whatever management expertise she could and took the opportunity to invite him to a holiday family celebration in a part of the country where he had no kin and apparently no place else to go.

It was one thing for the *wife* of a seven-foot Knick—Mederia Webster—to show up at Michelle's house. But an actual seven-footer? An active player? Michelle's young-adult and college-age children, already vacillating between bewildered and bothered by their mother's obsession with all things Knicks, initially didn't quite know what to make of this twenty-five-year-old African American from Beaumont, Texas, dropped suddenly into upper-middle-class white suburbia. They played the gracious hosts, peppering the soft-spoken Cavenall with abundant questions, hearing all about his unorthodox path to the Garden, all the while wondering why he had agreed to be there in the first place. But to Michelle, what was the big deal? Cavenall was just another acquaintance born of courtside access, another statement about her expanding social life in the big city. In the season of holiday spirit, why not bring home a dislodged Knick?

In spite of her Jewish roots and aversion to her Catholic grade-schooling, Michelle loved Christmas. The Muslers always celebrated with a tree and all the trimmings, conventionality making a rare visit to a most unconventional family. As her children ventured into young adulthood and spread around the country, Christmas was also an increasingly rare time they were all together. But once Michelle was entrenched at the Garden as a Knicks devotee, the holiday meal was served on Christmas Eve, conveniently scheduled to free her up to attend the traditional Knicks' Christmas Day game at the Garden.

By the time of the Cavenall visit, she had moved her family out of their old neighborhood and into a spacious ranch home on Rockridge Lane, a winding residential cul-de-sac hard off the Merritt Parkway in North Stamford. I, too, made the guest list at Michelle's new home, a couple of years after Beth and I were married. It was there that I saw a different side of my friend from the front row—a less self-assured side. At home, the maternal Michelle—not unlike most suburban mothers anxious about their children making a good impression on their invited guests—treaded carefully and sometimes clumsily with the five disparate personalities of her children, orchestrating the night as best she could and typically giving up along the way.

I didn't have to be around Michelle's kids long to see that they were all quite bright, bonded by a witty, acerbic dialogue, almost a language of their own—suggesting much time spent without a parent around to referee. When the dinner conversation inevitably turned to the Knicks, there was a fair amount of here-we-go-again eye-rolling, a collective reflex to the strange obsession they had long lived with, for better or worse.

For the boys, Brandon and Bruce, the two oldest, having the mom with the cool basketball tickets had had its benefit: an occasional game passed off to them and their friends. Bruce, in particular, enjoyed attending Knicks games as a high schooler in the late seventies. An accomplished athlete himself, he loved the game, along with the privilege of driving Michelle's sporty Datsun 280ZX home to Connecticut. The downside was her insistence on dragging him to the bar afterward to hang with the Garden in-crowd, munching on a late-night cheeseburger while she made the social rounds, leaving him exhausted the next morning and dozing through physics class.

In the mind of an adolescent girl uninterested in sports, on the other hand, Michelle's devotion to a pro basketball team made little sense. Devon, her middle daughter, wondered why her mother on occasion prioritized the Knicks over a school function, thinking, *Does she love the Knicks more than me?* The artistic Musler child, she preferred her ventures into the city with Michelle to the theater and museums. The Garden, not so much. Her memory of being dragged there for her birthday one year on a day they were handing out souvenir balls was a sour one; her mother, she decided, was "pimping me out for a ball she would give to my brother."

Whatever resistance there was at home to Michelle's love affair with the Knicks pretty much fell on deaf ears. She liked to say that the key to making an impact with people was to be a good listener—"be *interested* to be *interesting*," she would advise her kids and clients alike. But her children at times wondered if she was actually interested in listening to them as she made the Garden the center of her social universe, adding more hours away from home to her time spent at the office and on the road.

In retrospect, Blair, the youngest, saw an upside to her mother's basketball preoccupation: Michelle's absence from matters of maternal discipline. She considered the Knicks' schedule to be the family's authority surrogate of sorts—"the closest thing to a father figure." If a school event was scheduled on a night the Knicks were at home, the girls knew they shouldn't count on Michelle for transportation, much less attendance. But as Blair got older and less interested in her mother's involvement than her own independence, the Knicks' schedule also became "the greatest blueprint a teenager could ask for." It told her in advance what nighttime adventures she could get away with—even if she was grounded for trouble she'd already gotten into.

For her part, Michelle made no bones about the fact that she was more comfortable in the role of the typical dad—the career-oriented sports devotee with the best Knicks tickets. For almost all her life, it helped her to rationalize her absences and other parental flaws. A rare moment when she couldn't repress that guilt was triggered by, of all people, a basketball player. At home on her couch, she wept over a young multimillionaire giving thanks on national television to his mother.

In the spring of 2014, Kevin Durant, at a news conference in Oklahoma City to accept the NBA's Most Valuable Player trophy, gazed at his sobbing mother, Wanda Durant, in the audience and said, "You kept us off the street. You put clothes on our back. Food on the table. When you didn't eat, you made sure we ate. You went to sleep hungry. You sacrificed for us. You're the real MVP."

ESPN rewound the clip on a *SportsCenter* loop, and Michelle watched it again and again, tearing up each time. She knew why the connection was so meaningful, so poignant—and why she was steadfastly taken with the backstories of Durant and LeBron James, the best players of the twenty-first century, who habitually paid tribute to their mothers, their singular saviors through thick and thin. Secretly, Michelle fantasized about such a tribute from her own children—for toughing it out, staying the course. There was one catch, though. She never directly asked or lobbied for such acknowledgment because on a deep-seated level, unlike the single basketball moms she so admired, she didn't think she deserved it.

"I was never there for them," she told me during the 2017 holiday season, in what was a rare rumination, "and now it's too late."

For most of the time I had known Michelle, she made matter-of-fact, passing references to all that she hadn't done as a parent, all that she'd missed while working and playing. She would listen to me prattle on about my trials, tribulations, and triumphs with two growing boys—how for years I had exhausted myself rushing home from one road trip or another for a weekend soccer game or a birthday party—and invariably say, "I did none of that. I never had time."

She of course had a reason—or rationalization—for all she hadn't done as a parent. Working mom by day, devoted fan by night, she believed that she needed to keep changing, growing, because her career—and by extension her kids' lives—depended on it. Who would they have, she worried, if something happened to her? So much already had—illness, divorce, near-impoverishment.

"I was obsessed with making money, keeping the house, and one way to do that was to be socially engaged, connected to the right people," she said. She was convinced that her fluency in speaking the language of the game had helped her navigate a world of sports-obsessed men. O. B. Gray, a marketing executive at Warner who lived in Stamford and often rode the train home with Michelle, said she indeed had a "celebrity aura in the office," as the woman with the prize Knicks seats and access to the stars.

For much of her adult life, Michelle had accepted the trade-offs and terms of her reconstructed social life—the cards she'd been dealt, or played. Her children grew up, found partners, moved away, and led productive lives. For Michelle, the games continued, one season blurring into the next. She loved sports because she always thought a single game, segmented into stages, was a microcosm of life, with a beginning, a middle, and an end. But in life's twilight, and especially in the aftermath of another ministroke, she began to take inventory, to fret over what she had to show for what really mattered—or should have mattered—most.

What did all her game notes packets, programs, lanyards, and ticket stubs mean now? What would her children do with her profligate indulgences except toss them out with the trash when she was gone? "I keep thinking that there is no way to measure that family part," she said. "There is no final score, so what have I accomplished?"

Rationally, Michelle knew that she had been the MVP of her family—but only if the *P* stood for "provider." She'd given her children upper-middle-class stability and a first-rate education. She happily paid for all the tutors and coaches. Her pride about providing was never more palpable than when her adult daughter Blair had fallen seriously ill in Southern California, collapsing in a Target store and requiring two days of blood transfusions, eight hours of surgery, two months of hospitalization, six weeks of radiation, and five months of chemotherapy. Enduring more pain than she had ever imagined possible, more vulnerable than she'd ever been, Michelle nonetheless was stunned when the male oncologist appeared to be ignoring her in their consultation, maintaining eye contact with her ex-husband. Her fear turned to fury.

"Talk to *me*," she snapped, wanting to scream that she, not he, was the one who had sacrificed, who had suffered. Yet she was inescapably left with the self-judgment that she could have, or should have, done more.

Based on my knowledge of Michelle's family, I would argue with her that it was plainly obvious to any objective observer that her children were fine, out in the world, doing their thing. Her Christmas letters were annually filled with dutiful updates on their academic, athletic, and later professional and personal triumphs, along with the good-natured needling of a woman who at that time could reason that there were hard choices that had to be made—for their financial security and her own sanity, as she wrote in 1972:

Speaking of children—mine—they are so inconsiderate and selfish. They actually expect and want three meals a day. They even ask for clean clothes and sometimes they have the audacity to want things ironed. I keep telling them that there are children in Europe who would consider TV dinners a delicacy. Besides, I defrost better than any other mother on the block. I tell them that living with a star can be difficult but it will be a rewarding experience when they write their autobiographies: Life With Mother. I get the feeling they're unimpressed. 'Mother Who?' Devon asked the other day.

I wondered why in the world at this late stage of life she would blame herself—and for what, exactly? But it wasn't really blame, she said. It was more sadness. Because whatever I thought of her life from the outside looking in, she didn't have the same faith that her children, from inside the web of familial complexity, applied the same logic.

"They're not thinking, *Oh, my mother's wonderful because my father didn't do this or that*," she said. "I think they're thinking, *She was never here. She was out at a game somewhere or lying in bed, exhausted, and every time I was excited about something and tried to tell her about it, she didn't care*."

I told her that she would have been irate with me had I been the one reflecting so negatively, so despondently. Should I start to call her Woody-ana? But I also realized that we were at different stages of life; there were feelings running through her I couldn't yet comprehend, and this was a debate I wasn't about to win.

Not yet, anyway.

. . . .

As the holidays approached in 2017, Michelle found herself with an offer from Wynn Plaut, who had called to say she could have his tickets to the Knicks' annual Christmas Day game, against the Philadelphia 76ers, if she could figure out a way to get into the city. Knowing she hadn't been to a game since our trip together early in the season, I figured she would jump at the chance. But she sighed and said, "Probably not."

"Why not?" I asked during one of our Sunday phone conversations, my standard check-in time with Michelle after the morning political news shows we both watched.

"I'm thinking, maybe if you're out, you should really be out," she said, sounding tired, distracted, even dejected. She told me that she found herself to be "losing interest" in things, lamenting her difficulty in shaking morning cobwebs and needing to focus harder to follow shows on television and comprehend the more challenging stories in the papers. I reminded her that she was only weeks removed from the tests that her son Brandon had convinced her to take to affirm that she was still fit to drive. There had been two phases, physical and cognitive.

"You passed them both," I said.

"I know," she said. "But what's on my mind all the time now is letting go. Just letting go."

It was strange, and sad, to hear Michelle sound so despairing. She had been so hopeful just before Thanksgiving, after undergoing a spinal tap, during which her neurologist had drained a buildup of fluid from the brain with the intention of installing a shunt to create a permanent flow. The shunt, in turn, would decrease the chance of swelling and potentially improve Michelle's balance and mental acuity. But while fluid was drained, her doctors told her that she wasn't a candidate for the more complicated insertion of a shunt. She initially shrugged off the results: "Nothing ventured, nothing lost."

Now, suddenly, she was talking about *letting go*—in effect, giving up. Why? Had Michelle actually deteriorated, or was she merely having difficulty summoning the energy and positivity to carry on as usual? I knew how much she missed the Garden and couldn't help but wonder if finally surrendering her tickets, being severed from the identity that had strategically served her life's social reconstruction, was weighing heavily on her.

This, after all, was a loyalist who had once bragged to me for a 1990 *Daily News* column I wrote about her Knicks fidelity how she had cut short a work assignment in Hong Kong and endured twenty-eight exhausting hours of flights and layovers to make it to her seat for a playoff game against the Celtics. A woman who wasn't too embarrassed to write in one of her Christmas letters that if she could change anything about her life, which was largely about business and basketball, it would be to make basketball her business. In another Christmas missive, she even joked—at least we thought—that she "hopes to be buried" in her courtside seat "when the time comes."

In the years after her professional retirement, section 6 had been Michelle's virtual office, the place that had made her feel most vital, alive, connected to people she deemed important and admired: the broadcaster Mike Breen. The Garden icon Walt Frazier. The occasional opposing coach—including Doc Rivers of the Los Angeles Clippers and Scott Brooks of the Oklahoma City

Thunder and later the Washington Wizards, both of whom she had befriended during the brief periods they had played for the Knicks.

At the risk of overplaying my armchair psychology, I wanted to believe that Michelle was pulling what she would have called "a Harvey"—merely feeling sorry for herself, missing her many Garden friends and acquaintances. That at least was a more preferable diagnosis than the alternative, and it made sense that the narrowing of her life—as she had referred to it during our drive to the Garden in late October—would have had some psychological effect.

With the exception of Brandon, who lived in Manhattan, Michelle's children were scattered around the country—two in California, one in Florida, another in New England. Her grand-children had transitioned into busy, young-adult lives. Her best friends from the Garden—Drucie De Vries and Ernestine Miller—had moved on from her courtside perch, and checked in only with an occasional call. She'd lost a valued yoga partner when Robin Kelly moved to Manhattan after her divorce from Wynn Plaut.

To a much lesser degree, I could relate to the vacuum cre-ated by sudden vocational—or avocational, in Michelle's case—detachment. In the year-plus time since I had taken the buyout from the *Times*, many of the people with whom I had watched countless games, dragged myself through airports, and stood around sweaty locker rooms had pretty much vanished as quickly as I could sign the papers to collect my pension.

It was an emotionally jarring experience—more so than I had anticipated—to step off the carousel and watch it spin on while few, if any, bothered to wave. I did have the good fortune of being able to occasionally leap back on, continuing to contribute to the newspaper and so clinging to my perceived relevance, even as I berated myself for not yet trying new things.

Michelle was no shut-in either. Her neurological condition notwithstanding, she rarely missed a yoga class—what she called her "lifeblood"—or an opportunity to limber up in the gym. She made lunch dates, took herself to the movies, and looked forward to the limousine ride into the city for the occasional School of Visual Arts board meeting. But what happens when age, anxiety, and depression conspire to impede such pleasurable distractions? When an encroaching dread mixed with more isolation than usual creates the sensation of being, as Michelle described it, "slowly sucked into a void"?

Worried about her state of mind, I drove up to Stamford a few days after our phone conversation, the week before Christmas. Over dinner, I asked if she had reached the point where she needed help attending to daily . . . *things*. Was it time, perhaps, to reach out more, specifically to her children? She was adamant that it wasn't.

"All they would do is worry, and what does that accomplish?" she said, reminding me once again that her family relationships were complicated, with baggage from the past that, for her, was too difficult to pry open.

A close friend in the area, then?

There were, she said, a couple of people in her condominium mews she knew she could count on in an emergency. But no one she particularly wanted to burden on any regular basis—which, she argued, was still entirely unnecessary and would only risk their willingness to help out in a pinch.

"Friendships dissipate because most are of convenience in the first place," she said. "And from my age, you look back and wonder, who *were* your real friends?" She laughed and added, "You just need about ten more years and a few more good ones to die and you'll realize how few of them you actually had."

As fatalistic as that was, I at least knew that Michelle considered our friendship to be not just one of the good ones, but one of the better ones—and at this point in her life, perhaps the best one, even if it was a status I had reached by default. It nonetheless made me feel as if it was my responsibility to help get her out of her funk, as she had often done for me.

Over dinner, I pressed her on the Christmas tickets, knowing it had always been one of her favorite days of the season. Christmas traffic into the city most years was light and her second ticket usually went unsold, enabling her to show off a child, or in later years, a grandchild. No matter how badly the season was going, the Garden was festive, and the Knicks typically were resolved to put up a fight for the nationally televised audience.

More than thirty years earlier, on Christmas night 1984, Michelle and I had witnessed one of the greatest individual performances at the Garden: Bernard King's then-record sixty points in a losing cause against the New Jersey Nets. I covered the game as the beat reporter for the *Daily News*, writing on the usual tight nighttime deadline. Michelle waited for me to finish downstairs at the bar, which was buzzing with elation over the Knicks' good fortune of finally having a legitimate superstar—at twenty-eight, right in his prime—around which to build.

If there was one player who bridged whatever evaluative differences there may have been between fan and reporter, it was the Brooklyn-born King, hands down. We could argue about which other player was the greatest Knick of all—she would anoint Willis Reed, I would counter with Walt Frazier, and we both would give honorable mention to Patrick Ewing. But Michelle considered King to be the one and only Knick worth the price of admission every single night he suited up, and I once claimed in print that he was among the rarest of players anywhere I would have paid my way in to see (fortunately, nobody took me up on the offer).

As it happened, in the fall of 2017 King had released an autobiography, and soon after, an email arrived from a bookstore owner in Maplewood, New Jersey, asking me to moderate a Q&A session. After I agreed, my first call was to Michelle, who surmised, "You'll have to read the book, then, won't you?"

I could tell her curiosity was piqued. Michelle was always of the mind that King, more than any single player she had watched closely from behind the Knicks bench, had a compelling story to tell—and possibly some deep, dark secret to go along with it.

King was a comet streaking across the New York sky, a roughly three-season phenomenon that all but ended with the devastating collapse of his right knee late in the 1984–85 season, in which he was dominating opponents, averaging a career-high 32.9 points per game. Yet from the day in October 1982 that he reintroduced himself to his hometown until that cruel stroke of fate, there was no one quite like him. No one as electric, enigmatic, and complex. Who could forget Bernard and his terrifying Game Face (which, predictably, was the name of his book)? It was a mask of simmering rage mysteriously summoned from the moment he stepped onto the floor—a fearsome sight, even for courtside fans and reporters, akin to the early moments of a horror film before the spilling of first blood.

"Scared the shit out of me," Michelle said. "But he was so spectacular, so exciting, that you didn't even have to remember who won the game because he overshadowed everything else."

If the King era could be distilled into one game other than the Christmas sixty, it would have to be the night of April 27, 1984, in the decisive fifth game of the first-round playoff series against Isiah Thomas and the Detroit Pistons. It began at Joe Louis Arena in downtown Detroit with a ventilation system gone faulty. By the middle of the first quarter, everyone on the court—and those of us reporting at courtside—was drenched in sweat.

A furious pace made it sweatier. Led by King, the Knicks appeared to have a comfortable lead going down the stretch, until Thomas, the smallest man on the floor, erupted to score an almost unfathomable sixteen points in just over ninety seconds. With the game tied, he also had the ball for a potential game winner. But Darrell Walker, a rookie Knicks guard with exceptionally quick hands, stripped him in the lane. The game went to overtime, where King completed a 44-point night and a record 213 points for a five-game series in a 127–123 victory.

To the very end of my full-time sportswriting career, I considered that game to be as extraordinary as any I'd covered. Michelle called it the best Knicks game she'd ever seen, even if it was from her living room couch. The next time we spoke, she called me a "lucky SOB" for having watched it from courtside in Detroit.

Those of us in the building that night would argue that King was, for that series and season, as unstoppable an offensive force as any non-center they'd seen pre–Michael Jordan. But in the start to my *Daily News* story the following morning, Darrell Walker shared the heroism: "Bernard King stole our hearts. Isiah Thomas nearly stole the game. But Darrell Walker stole the ball."

It was the kind of multilayered lede I was proud of, integrating characters both central and secondary to develop an all-encompassing angle that could be expounded upon in the body of the story. In large part, I owed it to Michelle. She had been telling me all season how bad she felt for Walker, how he had become a continual target of Hubie Brown's ire, who had objected to Walker's selection in the draft. Armed with that information, I had the perfect opportunity to explore a rich irony: In what arguably was the most memorable victory of Brown's NBA coaching career, he was saved by a player he had little use for.

These were the inside stories that intrigued Michelle, who was never interested in mythical portrayals of players, in making them larger than life. She cared more about why and how they overcame their environmental circumstances, their human frailties—much like the power brokers she dealt with in her work. No Knick she watched so up close and personal better fit the profile or was more interesting in that psychological vein than King, with whom I'd had my differences over the years based on one column or another.

But a source of pleasant surprises in a long career in sports journalism is the ability to reconnect later in life with athletes you once covered—old wounds healed, scars faded, leaving aging adversaries with no need to hang on to hostility. At the bookstore, King and I hugged it out, and I moderated and re-corded the Q&A and got it published on a new sports website, The Athletic. I sent Michelle a copy and she emailed me the next day.

LOVED THE INTERVIEW WITH BERNARD AND FINALLY LEARNING
WHERE THE GAME FACE CAME FROM!!!

That was the news takeaway from King's book: His game face had been a defense mechanism, a veneer of defiance to the beatings he had regularly taken as a child from his mother. I wrote her back: "Now *that* is a mother who should have some regrets!"

When I called her a few days later, she had a pleasant surprise for me: She had decided to take the Christmas Day tickets after all, thanking me for talking her into it. Perhaps it was the King remembrances—Christmas game and all—that had triggered her holiday spirit. Michelle's Christmas Eve parties had ended years ago, but an invitation for dinner with her son, daughter-in-law, and granddaughter at their Manhattan apartment no doubt helped convince her to take Plaut's tickets. Christmas with her families, the Knicks and the Muslers, was too tempting a proposition. She asked Robin Kelly to meet her at the Garden and shelled out eighty dollars for a limousine into the city.

In the years after my children were born, we had established our own holiday tradition—Christmas with Beth's family at her sister's house in a suburb of Boston. Tuning in from there, I pointed out to Alex and Charly the familiar face behind the bench, returned to her perch. "My Michelle," I told them, smiling. That was how she had long been known around our house, from the time the boys were young and had happened to have a sitter with the same name.

Your Michelle. *My* Michelle.

All told, Michelle's day at the Garden had been exhausting. Making the trip to the arena from Stamford and navigating to her seat were taxing enough, and she was exasperated when Robin misplaced her wallet and needed help gaining entrance into the Garden. The next day, she felt the effects of a long day in the city. But she also had to admit, even after the Knicks had lost a close one to the Philadelphia 76ers, that it had felt good, very good, to be back.

Hearing Michelle talk about the Garden reinforced to me how important it was for her to still have occasional access. The arena was an entirely natural place for her to spend a holiday, a place where she could, for a few precious hours, feel connected, secure, holding on to hope—the Knicks' and her own.

I asked her if she still was thinking about cutting ties, letting go.

"No," she said. "I feel like I'm going to hang on for as long as I can."

It was exactly what I wanted—and needed—to hear.

Six

Old Friends and Bookends

On the afternoon of May 12, 1985, Michelle and I both had cause for jubilation when Dave DeBusschere, the Knicks' championship-era icon turned general manager, rose halfway from his seat in a ballroom at the Waldorf-Astoria Hotel in Manhattan and gently punched the air in triumph. He and the Knicks had just won the NBA's inaugural draft lottery with its much-heralded prize, Patrick Ewing.

My friendship with Michelle by this time was close in ways that transcended basketball. But seldom did the state of the Knicks *not* come up in our many conversations—on the phone or over long breakfasts at a diner near the Greenwich-Stamford border on weekends Beth and I spent out of the city with her parents. And in the half decade Michelle and I had known each other, there had been no bigger development, no greater newsbreak, than the Knicks landing Ewing, who was supposedly the second coming of Bill Russell, the hub of the Boston Celtics' unmatchable dynasty of the fifties and sixties. An intimidating seven-footer who had dominated opponents during his four years at Georgetown, Ewing was considered a virtual lock to lift the Knicks from the rash of injuries—most notably Bernard King's—that had dropped them to the depths of the league standings. If Ewing was to become even half as successful as Russell—winner of eleven titles in thirteen years—the Knicks stood to go on a joyride that would include multiple championship parades.

Because all seven lottery participants—the teams that had not qualified for the playoffs during the 1984–85 season—had had the same percentage chance of winning, cries of the fix being in quickly arose, never to be proven or quelled. Could the league have actually rigged the lottery to resurrect its biggest media market? Years after the fact, Michelle and I agreed that the conspiracy theories were preposterous, if only because David Stern, in only his second year as the NBA commissioner, would have been out of his mind to position his league one whistleblower from forfeiture of its credibility. But that was the business pragmatist (Michelle) and the journalist (me) who didn't want to believe the sport we were so invested in might not be competitively authentic. More from the heart, Michelle had boldly and wishfully assured friends and family in her Christmas letter months earlier that the Knicks—by hook or by crook—would wind up with Ewing. And on the day of the lottery, I filed a column to the *Daily News*, noting that the accounting firm in charge of the lottery's security just happened to represent the corporation that owned Madison Square Garden.

Whatever the truth was, Michelle (the fan) didn't much care. While the Garden's phone lines were jammed with requests for tickets, she was sitting pretty with orchestra seats for what promised to be Broadway's hottest and longest-running show. "I'm pinching myself," she said when I called from a phone bank in the lobby of the Waldorf after finishing my work that day, Mother's Day. Meanwhile, the fatalist in me just had to cause trouble. I reminded Michelle that the King injury, occurring just weeks earlier, had left a cloud over the potential King-Ewing pairing and by extension the franchise.

"If only Bernard hadn't gotten hurt," I told her.

"Would you *please* let me enjoy this?" she said.

The truth was, my naysaying was a complete act—I was as giddy as she. After spending the majority of my playoff springs in Boston, Los Angeles, and other league outposts, here was the possibility that New York City would soon become the center of the NBA universe. Not only would it spare me incessant travel, but what a story that would be to cover, the resurrection of the team I had idolized as a kid.

But the next few years didn't unfold as we had envisioned. For starters, Ewing never did represent the individual star power Larry Bird and Magic Johnson had already brought in tandem to the NBA, and certainly not the enhanced version that Michael Jordan would singularly define in the years ahead. He was no driver of overpriced sneakers and soft drinks. Worse, Ewing struggled with knee tendinitis over the first two seasons, King's rehab dragged on for almost all of them, and the franchise suffered from internal turmoil. Behind the scenes, Hubie Brown busily undercut DeBusschere, deflecting blame from himself for the team's poor record. When DeBusschere was fired, Brown bullied his replacement, Scotty Stirling, into sacrificing precious draft assets for stopgap transactions in hopes of saving his job. When that tactic failed and Brown was canned sixteen games into the 1986–87 season, the Knicks played on feebly until March 17, a day that began amid renewed hope: The recalcitrant, rehabilitating King showed up for his first workout with the team since his injury two years earlier.

Reality harshly intruded that night at the Garden. Ewing picked a bad time to have one of the worst games of his nascent career. The Knicks were blown out by the Denver Nuggets, who had lost seven straight games. The fans booed lustily while derisively chanting for Ewing to be replaced by Eddie Lee Wilkins. And then it really got ugly. The Knicks had handed out life-size posters of their young center, which restless fans began using to fashion rolled-up projectiles. One idiot slipped past security, appeared at courtside, and tore his poster to shreds. Michelle watched this unfold grimly from her courtside seat, the game delayed as ball boys cleared the floor of the promotional debris.

"The worst thing I've ever seen there," she said, adding that she would never forget the sadness on Ewing's normally stoic face. Indeed, it might well have been the most embarrassing chapter in the history of a fan base long touted as the most respectful of the game, but it was also a fair representation of a franchise with a growing knack for self-sabotage, or just rotten timing and luck. Within a few weeks, King returned to play the final six games of the season, but Ewing and his tender knees had already been shut down. The two never played a single minute together.

By summer, the Knicks had a new general manager, Al Bianchi, who wanted to hire a veteran coach but was told that ownership preferred Rick Pitino, a rising star at Providence College in Rhode Island, who had briefly served as an assistant with the Knicks under Hubie Brown. One of their first personnel decisions was to disavow any allegiance to King, who moved on to Washington, only to eventually regain his All-Star status. Initially, Bianchi and the relentlessly energetic Pitino did breathe fresh air into a stale Knicks environment. Their best acquisition was a much-needed point guard via the draft. The flamboyant and New York–bred Mark Jackson became the key that unlocked Ewing's offensive gifts, which turned out to be more formidable than anyone had expected, and certainly superior to Bill Russell's. Michelle immediately fell hard for Jackson, who won Rookie of the Year and helped the Knicks sneak into the 1988 playoffs, where they lost a spirited first-round series to Bird and the Celtics. She adopted as a mantra a line from my *Daily News* column. Jackson, I wrote, had done what Ewing had not: "turned the lights on at the Garden." It was less a criticism of Ewing than it was a hat tip to the value of a crafty passer and charismatic personality.

With Jackson leading and Ewing dominating, the Knicks won more games in the second year of the Bianchi-Pitino regime, 1988–89, than they had since their second and last championship season sixteen years earlier. They entered the playoffs as potential contenders. But there were fissures in the relationship between Bianchi and Pitino. For two years, Bianchi had begged Pitino to incorporate a more detailed half-court offense to complement his preferred fast-break attack, which was triggered by a pressing defense. Pitino resisted what he perceived as front-office interference. Bianchi was proved right when Michael

Jordan and the Bulls slowed the game tempo and eliminated the favored Knicks from the second round of the playoffs in six games. But Pitino got the last laugh, landing the premier college job at Kentucky that a bitter Bianchi believed he'd been angling for all along.

Without Pitino, the team's growth spurt stalled. The city's enthusiasm waned. The brief love affair with Jackson cooled. Even before Pitino left town, the fans had begun to sour on the point guard, booing his shot selection in the first two playoff games against the Bulls. He answered like the headstrong New Yorker he was, condemning his critics as "rats deserting a sinking ship." Then he braced for an onslaught of derision when the teams returned to the Garden from Chicago.

He heard it from nearly everyone, but not Michelle, who stood up for her man as boos rained down with a handmade sign that read: JAX'S RATS—WE NEVER LEAVE THE SHIP. A photographer from the *Daily News* took notice, landing Michelle on the next day's back page. It earned her a new friend—seldom was there a home game after that episode when Jackson's mother, Marie, failed to stroll across the floor before tip-off to give her son's most loyal fan a hug. Their friendship carried over to the postgame bar and an occasional lunch. Mark Jackson, who would much later coach the Golden State Warriors and become a popular analyst on the NBA's lead broadcast team, would never forget Michelle's support. "The fact is that I still get a chill thinking about her standing up for me when everyone else in the building was booing," he told me three decades later.

The idea of kicking the Knicks when they were down was always anathema to Michelle. What did the fans think that would get them? How would they feel about being booed on their jobs? In retrospect, she also recognized the Ewing and Jackson fiascos as flash points in her understanding of how the Garden fans were really a reflection of the team's notoriously capricious ownership. They behaved erratically because that was how the franchise typically conducted its business.

Any human resources executive worth her weight would know how counterproductive it was for the Knicks to have settled on Pitino as coach before choosing Bianchi as general manager. It was the same executive malpractice the Knicks had committed when pairing Dave DeBusschere and Hubie Brown. The smart play, Michelle kept reminding me for my stories, was to avoid shotgun marriages by allowing the highest-level basketball executive to choose his subordinates, thereby creating a chain of command that was built on loyalty and trust. Unfortunately for the Knicks and their fan base, Michelle was never asked to consult on personnel decisions. It was no surprise that front office cohesion and collaborative effort were rare there, where watching one's back was in itself a competitive sport. This infighting frustrated Michelle more than what actually happened on the court. She began to fear that she might be sitting behind the bench for the rest of her life without ever seeing her team win. From my courtside press row seat and in my columns for the *Daily News*, I was wondering about that myself.

The New Year, 2018, was only a few days old when a call came from a *Times* editor wondering if I was interested in profiling Ewing, whose post-playing career had taken a fascinating turn: He was now the head coach at Georgetown University, his alma mater. I accepted the assignment without hesitation and immediately called Michelle to tell her I was heading to Washington, D.C. "Of course you should write that story," she said. I had covered so many twists and turns of Ewing's career, so why not the latest one?

The progression from player to coach has historically been a more likely career track for charismatic players, often point guards, well-practiced as they are in both verbal and tactical on-court leadership. You could practically tag and identify a future coach by the sound of his voice in media interviews—personable, polished, imperturbable, and generally self-promoting. But until very late in his playing days, Ewing's was deliberately muted, his leadership evidenced almost exclusively by the weight of his much-admired work ethic. He came off as reticent, distant, deliberately dull. He honored minimum media requirements but stonewalled reporters in most other ways. He was allergic to schmoozing with them before a game and never seemed to have a favorite media confidant. Until late in his career, he hardly ever addressed any of us by name.

As unreachable as he was for those of us scavenging for a quote, Ewing was just as remote to the Knicks' fan base at large—even to those, like Michelle, who on a regular basis across the years were practically in his face. Never shy about using her proximity to establish a rapport with coaches, players, and assorted others, she found Ewing's invisible shield to be impenetrable. She could never get him to interact, not so much as a smile or a nod. Was Ewing just locked in on the task at hand? Indifferent? Uncaring? Too shy? Understandably distrustful of outsiders after the racist taunting he endured as a high school prodigy in the Boston area and to a lesser degree at Georgetown?

Teammates and opposing players sang a different tune about Ewing. They raved about his easy demeanor, his mischievous sense of humor. At the 1992 Summer Olympics in Barcelona, he developed a teasing friendship with Larry Bird—an improbable bond between a black native Jamaican and the white "Hick from French Lick," the small Indiana town from where Bird hailed.

This charming side of Ewing was strictly hearsay to Michelle and to me until Lori Hamamoto, a Knicks employee, convinced her—and by extension, us—otherwise. Hamamoto had come to the Knicks from the public relations team of the Orlando Magic and, after serving time in New York as an assistant, was promoted in 1996 to communications director. It was an impressive ascent for someone in her late twenties and even more notable for a woman in the male-dominated sports industry. More than most, Michelle took notice. With no relationship with Hamamoto to speak of, she walked up to her one game night and handed her a note, offering congratulations and the advice to continue pushing through glass ceilings. Hamamoto appreciated that someone she correctly assumed to be a successful career woman—what else would explain her choice seat location without a leveraged man by her side?—had taken the time to contemplate her success, much less go out of her way to acknowledge it. In the way Michelle had connected to others at the Garden, including me, a close friendship resulted, lasting long after Hamamoto's departure from the Knicks in 2001.

With her own family a day trip away in the Washington area, Hamamoto would periodically take the train to Stamford from

Grand Central Station and look for Michelle's vanity license plate—always some abridged version of her first name—in the parking lot. When the two were out to dinner, Michelle would introduce her as her "adopted daughter" because Hamamoto was actually young enough to be her daughter. Their relationship was also—however abstractly—another example of Michelle's journalist's instincts leading her to information that was otherwise unavailable. In her time with the Knicks, Hamamoto had developed a close working friendship with Ewing. Her loyalty and professionalism would have never allowed her to reveal any secrets, but she would on occasion tout behind-the-scenes gestures unknown to reporters because Ewing had no interest in making them public and certainly not in going out of his way to ingratiate himself with the media. Michelle, in turn, would pass along these insights to me, which helped to humanize him in my columns.

In her early days in the director's job, Hamamoto was understandably cautious around me, a *Times* columnist who had taken my fair share of shots at Ewing—most aggressively for clumsily handling a management lockout that delayed the 1998–99 season as president of the players' union. Hamamoto wasn't pleased with the column and mentioned it to Michelle. Determined to bring her friends together, Michelle arranged a dinner, where I explained to Hamamoto that, labor criticism aside, I admired Ewing and, in fact, had vigorously defended him during leaner times earlier in his career. I also told her that I would never evaluate any athlete based on his cooperation—or lack thereof—with the media. That was the last thing readers cared about. We reached an understanding, forged our own friendship, and through the years would plan the occasional dinner in Stamford with Michelle. "WONDERFUL MEMORIES WITH TWO PEOPLE I LOVE," Michelle emailed me after one such outing.

Once I had the D.C. assignment, the first person I reached out to after Michelle was Hamamoto, who had, not surprisingly, joined Ewing in Washington to help launch his program as its communications director.

"Need to speak with you," I texted her.

"Please tell me it's not about Michelle," she answered, immediately worried it was health related. On the phone, I assured her that Michelle, relatively speaking, was fine, though undoubtedly a little jealous that we would be spending time together without her.

At Georgetown, Ewing greeted me with a bro hug, another example, as with Bernard King, of time and no doubt age having smoothed over the rough edges of our professional relationship. After so many years, we were bonded by the journey, not by any lingering memories or resentments over anything I had written.

When my story ran soon after the New Year, I tweeted a link to it with an insouciant heading: "Went to see Patrick Ewing. Think he was actually happy to see me!" A tweet back from Ewing appeared on my feed the next day: "Always happy to see a fellow Hall of Famer." I drove up to Stamford soon after New Year's and wasted no time showing off the tweets to Michelle, for whom Twitter was a mystery world she would never visit on her own. She guffawed in delight.

"Never thought I'd live to see the day," she said.

M y Ewing story was timed with a purpose, a New York angle, with Ewing bringing his Georgetown team to Madison Square Garden to play St. John's University. It was a reunion, a homecoming, and a turf war all wrapped into one Big East Conference coaching showdown between Ewing and Chris Mullin, long-ago antagonists for these same Catholic schools during the early to mid-eighties and longtime subjects of my columns. Writing about them in tandem—this time as the best of frenemies—was an ideal career symmetry, and they playfully hyped the occasion.

"Chris knows that it's my house," Ewing teased, citing his number 33 Knicks jersey hanging from the rafters as proof. A call to Mullin yielded this game but prickly response: "I grew up there and came back. Patrick was put there by the NBA."

Even as he spent his Hall of Fame pro career on the West Coast (Golden State Warriors) and in the Midwest (Indiana Pacers), Mullin was a native son of Brooklyn with a classic Irish mug, pasty white in a sport trending black. As a result, he was irresistible copy to my tabloid editors at the *Post* and *Daily News*, always fixated on endless speculation that he might return home to play for the Knicks. Our respective career beginnings had been nearly simultaneous, timed for me to report on Mullin as a high school hoops prodigy and then a St. John's superstar along the way to a climactic college career appearance—along with Ewing's Georgetown Hoyas—in the 1985 Final Four. His elevation to the NBA also coincided with my ascension from the Knicks beat at the *Daily News* to writing about the NBA at large. I happened to be on the job in Seattle one November night in 1985 when word circulated that Mullin would sign his first pro contract with the Warriors after a brief holdout and immediately make his pro debut. I took a dawn flight to Oakland, California, and sat with his proud parents, Rod and Eileen, at the introductory press conference, his tearful mother whispering to me that she wished her boy didn't have to be so far from home.

Our careers continued evolving. Our paths kept crossing. Three years later, I caught up with Mullin—by then a full-fledged NBA All-Star—in his condo just outside Oakland, where I had covered the first two games of the 1989 Bay Area World Series. As the series shifted to San Francisco for Game 3 on a calamitously fateful Tuesday evening, my editors in New York asked me to instead pursue a Mullin feature for an NBA season's preview. In my interview that afternoon with Mullin—hours before the tragic Loma Prieta earthquake would send me on an all-night vigil covering the collapse of a double-decker Oakland freeway— he shared in detail how his father, a recovering alcoholic, had supported him through his own very personal quake.

A year into Mullin's NBA career, he had landed in rehab after an admission of alcoholism he had dreaded to make for fear it would, as he told me, kill his father. Instead, Rod Mullin gave himself over to the cause of helping his son get and stay clean. When Mullin returned to the Warriors, playing in the Pacific time zone, late into the wee hours back east, his father stayed awake, awaiting his son's postgame call to talk about the game— and to make sure Chris's sobriety had survived another day.

Journalists store such information, suspecting there will come a time to use or reuse it. It was with that disclosure in mind that I drove out to see Mullin in Brookville, Long Island, on the morning of March 17, 1991, for what would be another fatefully timed meeting at the intersection of our careers and lives. He had lost his father six months earlier to cancer at age fifty-six, one year after I had buried mine following his heart attack at sixty-seven. We lounged in the family room of the house he had bought for his parents, a suburbanized upgrade from the cramped homestead in Brooklyn's Flatbush section, where the four brothers shared one bedroom and two bunk beds. The new digs had a pool and a basketball court, but all Mullin could dwell on was that his father had not lived long enough to enjoy it. Nor could he recall ever playing at Madison Square Garden without his father close by in the stands. "I guess," he said sadly, "this will be the first."

I, too, was thinking of my father with mixed emotions on a day of moving on. The interview with Mullin was my first assignment as a newly hired reporter for the *Times*. It had been an agonizing, soul-searching journey to the paper of record, the offer coming at the end of a five-month strike by members of the NewsGuild of New York and other unions at the *Daily News*.

In a thinly disguised effort to break the unions, the parent Tribune Company had continued publishing, eventually luring back a number of editors and reporters with threats of imminent permanent replacements. A few weeks into the strike, rationalizing that I needed to work to support my nearly year-old son and a pricey co-op apartment in Brooklyn Heights, I caved to that fear. Told by the paper's executive editor that he was soon to choose a permanent replacement for me, I crossed the line, wrote a column on the Knicks, and found it plastered with my photo the next morning at a neighborhood newsstand on the back page. A wave of nausea engulfed me. I left the paper on the newsstand, walked across the street, and vomited into a trash basket. I went back on strike, grateful, at least, that my father hadn't lived to see his son cross his union picket line.

He never did *get* my work the way Rod Mullin could relate to Chris's. Basketball is a relatively simple game—the ball goes into the basket or it doesn't. The team wins or it doesn't. But sports journalism was a mystery to a man who wasn't much interested in printed words and cared little about professional sports. Who went to work every day at the post office, valued his union as the deity, and lived by the doctrine that a picket line was sacred, never to be crossed. That didn't mean he wasn't proud of my byline, the evolution of the family lineage from barely literate immigrant (his father) to blue-collar working man to college-educated scribe. My father worked literally across the street from the Garden, but we walked in worlds that were nothing alike, though they intersected one summer day in the late eighties when he was walking along a Brooklyn neighborhood's commercial strip and came upon a crowd outside a store.

"What's going on?" he asked someone.

"Chris Mullin, the basketball player, is signing autographs," he was told.

Until the day he died, my father cut my stories from the paper and slipped them into the bottom drawer of his bureau. I suspect he didn't actually read much of them before he stored them. I'm certain that he had no idea who Chris Mullin was, but he got on line and waited to reach the front. "My son writes about basketball for the *News*," he said. Hearing my name, Mullin smiled.

"One of the best," he said, grabbing my father's hand, making a new fan.

At the Mullin home in Brookville, we reminisced about our fathers, the no-frills work (Rod Mullin had been a customs inspector at Kennedy airport) they did without fanfare, without complaint. When I left for the ride back into the city, I was contemplating the theme of a bittersweet Mullin homecoming for my story, when I was struck by the realization of how poignant that piece could be if I had also been making a return with the rest of the *Daily News* strikers, who happened to be going back on the job following the sale of the newspaper that very day.

The *Times*, I knew, would be happy to run my story on Mullin, but it would be just that: a story, lacking in any personal involvement. I, however, had been writing general columns at the *News* for a short while and was thinking like a columnist, not a reporter—driven by emotion, a spontaneous muse. The thought of returning to the *News* with my fellow strikers after five months of picket line duty, of shared fears of financial calamity, of careers prematurely dangling on the threshold of ruin, was suddenly quite tempting. Like Mullin's, my return would be bittersweet, the paper having lost some of its finest journalists, along with a healthy chunk of circulation. But the strikers, too, would be pushing forward through the pain of loss, moving on with life.

I suddenly questioned whether I wanted to or should leave the gritty tabloid, the working man's paper—my father's paper—for the upscale *Times*. I had a pretty good idea of what he would have wanted. Earlier in my career, while still at the *Post*, I had been invited to lunch by the *Times*'s sports editor for what turned out to be a courtesy introduction. Even a call from the august *Times* had seemed like something worth bragging about—except to my unimpressed, blue-collar father.

"Nobody reads that paper," he said with disdain.

Come again? Nobody reads the freaking *New York Times*? Not only deflated, I was embarrassed for him and mortified for myself—until I mentioned the conversation to Michelle. On the contrary, she thought his response was endearing, refreshingly honest, in no way crazy. "I bet in his world, in his neighborhood, he's absolutely right—nobody reads the *Times*," she said.

When I persisted in complaining about my family's being stuck in the proletarian mind-set and mud, with little sense of upward mobility and without interest in or appreciation of my work, she cut me off. She told me that she had once had similar feelings about her family but had long come to grips with her upbringing and even her father's bizarre double life. In young adulthood, she had grown a healthier respect for him, especially when she learned of the position of influence he had risen to in the steamfitters' union. Maybe her father didn't have the time or ability to mentor her into academia, but neither had he tried to quash her ambition of going to college when many other young women of her generation and class standing were nudged off to work or into marriage. And while her brother also became a steamfitter, her father had provided precious funds to help her pay for college.

"I don't know why you are waiting for your father or anyone in your family to give you something they are not capable of giving," Michelle said. "Especially when you can get that some-place else."

"You mean from you?" I said.

"OK, from me, and a lot of other people who took an interest in you because you had talent."

In the years after his death—better too late, I suppose, than never—I did come to appreciate how my father had, in his own way, inspired me. He got up at the crack of dawn every morning and commuted an hour and a half each way into Midtown. He sat at the kitchen table, his monthly bills laid out, stretching what he earned to meet his obligations. He passed along his work ethic without ever preaching to me about it. I've wondered many times whether I would have crossed the picket line had he been alive. I doubt it. I also know it would have made leaving the *Daily News* for the *Times*—the paper *he* read for the one that *nobody* read—even harder than it was.

On the drive into the city from the Mullin home on Long Island, I entered Manhattan on the East Side, a few blocks from the *News*'s old headquarters on Forty-second Street between Second and Third avenues. I drove over and parked behind the building. I sat in the car for a good half hour, more uncertain than I'd ever been about my career, my purpose, my place. I got out, walked to a street phone, and, like an addict dialing his sponsor, called Michelle to tell her that I was outside the *Daily News* and was considering going back in, hoping I could reclaim my job.

"*Oh?*" she said.

I told her about the interview with Mullin, the shared recollections of our fathers, the temptation I felt in my gut to hold on to the job that I'd spent the previous five months fighting for.

"For you or for your father?" she said. "Because if it's for him, how do you know that's what he would have wanted?"

"You remember what he said about the *Times*, don't you?"

"I do," she said. "But he didn't really read the stories in the *Post* or the *News* either. He bought them and saved them to show you that he cared."

I didn't have to ask Michelle for her opinion on which newspaper she thought I belonged at. I already knew. The sports-heavy tabloids could never have the heft of the *Times*, which she devoured front to back and considered the apex of journalism.

"You sound like you need permission from someone to do this," she said.

"Maybe I do," I said.

"Then go take it and don't look back," she said. "It's your life, not your father's. And if you think he wouldn't buy the *Times* and also cut out everything you write there, then you didn't know him very well."

I thanked her for hearing me out. In tears, but emboldened with newfound clarity, I walked back to the car and drove across town to the *Times* building on the West Side. As Michelle had insisted, I didn't look back.

Seven

. . . .

The New Good
Old Days

Hands down, the most insufferable Knicks fans are those who lived through the glory of the early seventies, who worshipped the legendary teams colloquially known as the "Old Knicks." Their fans—and count me among them—are forever lecturing their titleless descendants on the joys of authentic drama (Willis Reed limping out for Game 7 of the 1970 Finals) and *real* basketball (the selfless, find-the-open-man style of that two-title era).

For that aging crowd, even mentioning any contemporary Knicks team in the same breath as their Red Holzman–coached heroes is tantamount to comparing today's cable news pontificators to Walter Cronkite. Younger fans, deprived of championship parades, have had to settle for the brief period in which Bernard King was a sensation, the noble but ringless nineties, and, in the case of youngest and most deprived, the near destitution of the twenty-first century.

Michelle and I were part of a small faction that occupied the space between: We were fortunate to remember the title-winning teams of the seventies, but given how far away those true glory days felt, the nineties took on the status of the *new* good old days, a time in recent history that we felt we'd properly lived through and could feel proud of as fans and respectful of as journalists. Michelle had been a preoccupied mother of five and thus only a casual fan when the Knicks twice within four seasons overcame Jerry West, Wilt Chamberlain, and the Lakers to capture the franchise's first titles. But she had become a courtside fanatic by the time the nineties Knicks, under the coaching tutelage of Pat Riley and later Jeff Van Gundy, twice electrified the city with runs to the Finals. I was a high school– and college-age diehard when Reed was the team's heart and soul and Walt Frazier the king of cool. But I was an established insider just hitting the peak of my sports journalism career when Riley, Patrick Ewing, and company lugged the Knicks back onto center stage as a worthy adversary of Michael Jordan and the Chicago Bulls.

The hiring of Riley is commonly recalled as the birth of a sustained Knicks revival. But it was actually an intervention by David Stern, reflecting his backroom determination to resurrect the media-rich New York market, that pointed the Knicks in a new direction. Stern targeted the fractious front office, advocating for thirty-five-year-old Dave Checketts, who had broken into the league in the NBA's executive office and later with the Utah Jazz, to replace Al Bianchi as the Knicks' general manager. Blond, blue-eyed, and evincing a virtuous rectitude based on his Mormon faith, Checketts was a paradoxical personality for New York City. He nonetheless became the polished executive the franchise never had, luring Riley back into coaching after an unhappy year as a network television analyst and dragging a historically staid franchise into a new-age NBA.

Riley wasn't Checketts's only import with Los Angeles roots. As the 1991–92 season approached—my first at the *Times*—he announced the formation of the Knicks City Dancers, embracing the leggy pageantry conceptualized by Jerry Buss, the Lakers' playboy owner, with the Laker Girls at the dawn of the Magic Johnson/Showtime era in 1979. The prospect of dancers at the hallowed Madison Square Garden drew the immediate ire of at least one courtside traditionalist, who complained that time-outs and halftime "are for schmoozing" and took the opportunity to voice her sincere objections by mail to Checketts, copying me:

> *Dear David Checketts:*
>
> *When you reach the bottom of this letter, there will be a woman's signature there. DO NOT ASSUME that this has anything to do with a women's issue.*
>
> *This is a basketball issue. This is New York City. We know the game. We love the game. We go to the Garden to see THE GAME.*
>
> *DANCING GIRLS?????*
>
> *Tell me it isn't true. Not here, no way, no time, never, never, never.*
>
> *Put them in the Paramount with Barry Manilow, that's where they belong.*
>
> > *Sincerely,*
> > *Michelle Musler, Sept. 19, 1991.*

I immediately put the letter to good use, reprinting it in a column in which I fully agreed with Michelle while introducing her to my new *Times* readers. Checketts took note of it. When training camp commenced, while making his introductory rounds with the writers, he turned to me and asked, "This Michelle Musler—is she someone I need to know?"

Yes, I told him. Because she was as authentic and loyal a fan as he was going to find. Because she was an incorrigible letter writer on multiple matters—she once chastised the broadcaster Dick Schaap on the lack of racial diversity on his Sunday morning ESPN panel discussion show, *The Sports Reporters*. Checketts was likely to hear from her again, and again, and she also was certain to copy at least one member of the media on every letter she wrote. But at least on the subject of the City Dancers, her letter didn't deter Checketts because, well, no one else seemed to mind them too much. There certainly was no backlash from our newspaper pals, who had apparently been enjoying the eye candy at the Great Western Forum in Los Angeles and in other league venues going for glitz. In so many words, they told me I was nuts.

The reality was that professional basketball of the nineties was almost unrecognizable from its origins, the days of burly white men pounding on one another inside smoky gyms in forbidding winter outposts like Fort Wayne, Indiana, and Rochester, New York. In the eighties, Julius Erving, Larry Bird, and Magic Johnson had comprised the inaugural generation of genuine star power in the NBA. In the later eighties and nineties, Air Jordan would take the game's promotional potential to soaring heights. There was no turning back the clock, no resetting the blurring lines between entertainment and sports. In New

York, no one embodied this profound cultural shift more than Pat Riley. Checketts was an effective corporate front man, but Riley was—night in, night out—a star on the coaching front line, for all to behold.

He arrived in town with the coaching imprimatur of a champion four times over, a luminary right out of Hollywood casting. The stylized aura he created with the Lakers was mimicked in popular film, his slicked-back hair and aspirational certitude a harbinger of the fictitious Gordon Gekko from the 1987 blockbuster film *Wall Street*. Gekko's insatiable appetite for earning had nothing on the competitive ambitions of Riley, whose star was destined to shine even brighter in New York, where the Knicks had no Magic personality—only Patrick Ewing and his aversion to attention.

Riley's primary appeal was his aloof, serious style. He didn't even have to try very hard to attract the spotlight. Like Ewing, he was all business, not one to mingle with fans like Michelle. Over the four years Riley coached in New York, she could recall just two interactions. One game night, Ernestine Miller happened to notice a widening split on a back seam of Riley's sports jacket. But what to do? Riley was not readily approachable, and certainly not in the middle of a game. As he turned to walk off at halftime, the good women behind the iconic, *GQ*-cool coach waved to get his attention and told him that he'd probably want to know that his jacket was unraveling. He nodded coolly, returned for the second half wearing a different one, and thanked them. "That was probably the friendliest he ever was," Michelle said.

Not long after, at a promotional event at the NBA store, she encountered Riley and reminded him that she had been one of the sports jacket whisperers the night his seam split. He acknowledged her, but left it at that, as if the wardrobe malfunction needed to remain their little secret.

By then, Riley was above it all, virtual basketball royalty. On occasion, he dropped his guard exactly enough to allow us a glimpse beyond the pose to see just how big a celebrity he was. One night after a game, I wandered with a few colleagues into Elaine's, the Upper East Side hangout that attracted an eclectic mix of entertainers and journalists. By chance, we landed at a table next to Riley's; he was having a late meal with his wife, Chris, and the movie star couple Alec Baldwin and Kim Basinger. At one point, Riley surprised and flattered me, wisecracking to his actor friends, deliberately loud enough for me to hear, "Careful what you say, the *New York Times* is right behind you." That led to a brief introduction, which enabled me to shamelessly inform my wife the next morning that Basinger had blessed me with a smile.

Michelle, for her part, prided herself on trying not to be overly impressed by fame—but there were exceptions. Riley was one. Even she couldn't resist the persona he had so carefully cultivated. "He was just so beautiful to look at," she said, amazed by how he could make grand theater out of almost everything he did, without appearing to try.

It had taken all of four games in his first season at the Garden for both of us to see that the Knicks had tapped into something special. On the night of November 7, 1991, the world learned that Magic Johnson had tested positive for HIV and was retiring from the Lakers. I was driving into the city, heading to the Garden from my in-laws' home in Greenwich, when I heard on the radio the crushing news out of Los Angeles. Upon arrival at the arena, the first order of business had to be Riley's reaction.

In a gathering with reporters before the game against the Orlando Magic, he told us of a letter he had received from Johnson the previous day, presumably mailed before he had received the medical report. "Ironic, but he talked about the moments we had in the last ten years, and he wished me luck," Riley said, holding back tears. But it was what he did soon after that stole the night, and the Garden's heart. Before the opening tip, Riley summoned both teams to center court and took hold of a microphone to address the players and crowd together. He extoled Magic's "tremendous courage," his willingness to stand up that day at a news conference and "put his face right out front," the rare celebrity to match it to a disease still largely in the shadows. Then he brought the roughly two dozen players together and led them in quiet prayer. I turned to make eye contact with Michelle, who was crying. We all were, I suppose, given the gravity of what then sounded like a death sentence. And because Riley's grace and conviction made it difficult not to.

"You could see how devastated he was," Michelle said, recalling that night as one of her most disturbing but memorable behind the Knicks bench. She spent more time that night watching Riley trying to get through the night than she paid attention to the game.

Riley watching was a spectator sport in its own right at the Garden—what he was wearing on the sideline, how he commanded it, how he molded the Knicks during the course of one season from a team without great resolve to one that played a cantankerously physical brand of ball. From Michelle's privileged vantage point, even time-outs called by Riley were compelling, as she bragged in her 1992 holiday letter.

> *I am part of every team huddle. I pay more attention to Riley's orders than Greg Anthony, who watches the dancing girls, and Patrick Ewing, who watches the TV monitors, and John Starks, who is circling Mars. I know who broke the play and who is in the doghouse. I recognize every play called and am prepared to execute it should Riley call my number!*

With Riley driving them, the Knicks won fifty-one games in the 1991–92 season and defeated Isiah Thomas and the two-time-champion Detroit Pistons in the first round of the playoffs. Then they took on Jordan and the Bulls, who were defending their first title. They went into Chicago and won Game 1 behind Ewing's breakout performance. The series, suddenly competitive, turned into a nasty war of attrition and will. There was little the Knicks or anyone could do about Jordan, but Riley, like other coaches, believed the way to beat the Bulls was to bully their second-most-important player, Scottie Pippen. All series long, the Knicks' bruising forwards—Charles Oakley, Xavier McDaniel, and Anthony Mason—muscled and manhandled Pippen until John Starks, their talented but impulsive guard, took the strategy to extremes, slamming Pippen to the floor on a fast break during a heated Game 6 at the Garden.

By a quirk of logistical fate, my press row seat that night was on the far side from the Knicks bench, providing a nearly unobstructed view into the Bulls' huddle. After Starks's flagrant foul,

Pippen staggered to the bench, blood oozing from his nose. He was trailed by Jordan, who literally shoved Phil Jackson, their coach, aside and thrust a finger in Pippen's face.

"Next time you touch the ball, you drive it down their fucking throats or you'll answer to me," Jordan told his dazed teammate, with a controlled rage I had never seen. It was that kind of court-side access that made the NBA—in those days, at least—all the more compelling for reporters and readers, and unlike any other team sport.

Back in Chicago for Game 7, the Bulls pulled out the series but the Knicks had left an impression: This was no fluke. That's what Riley promised, and no one in New York was inclined to doubt him. Certainly not Michelle, who would send her season-ticket renewal package back with a check as soon as she received it, before the Knicks could change their mind and offer her location to someone else.

Beyond the sadness and fear on the night Riley and the Knicks prayed for Magic Johnson earlier that season was the eventual realization that the shocking announcement was also a measure of the NBA's ascendance. Almost a year before the Dream Team would become a global marketing sensation, Magic's retirement was worldwide news. The NBA mattered as never before, thanks to its telegenic stars and the shoe companies helping to elevate them to full-blown celebrity status—led by Nike, which had made Jordan the face of its burgeoning empire. In New York, the Knicks mattered because Riley, their leader, had fit them with an instant identity, one that belied his corporate look and mirrored the schoolyard jock he had been while growing up in a working-class family in Rome, New York.

These Knicks, aching to take Jordan down a peg or two, were going to be heard from again. Riley would have it no other way. Seven years after the Ewing draft lottery, Michelle believed the hottest show in town had finished its previews and was ready for a long, rewarding run. Having missed out on the championship years, with her time as a season-ticket holder closing in on two decades, she had every right to believe it was her due.

J ournalists root, too. Not in the tribal way that fans do, with unconditional allegiance to the cause or team colors. Sometimes it is the opposite, secretly and selfishly wishing a local team to fail early in the playoffs to lessen the workload. In 1985, for instance, I rooted for the Lakers-Celtics Finals to end quickly so I could get home and prepare for my wedding. In the 1993 Finals, Chicago's John Paxson hit a three-point shot to spare the Bulls a seventh game in Phoenix, also sparing Beth, who was eight months pregnant, having to close on the sale of a Brooklyn Heights co-op and the purchase of a home in Montclair, New Jersey, and move all on the same day by herself.

More often, we pull for the best story on any given day or over the course of a season. For a team's resurrection or redemption. For the unexpected rise or, yes, spectacular collapse. When the home team is the one making big news, the local buzz is louder. Newspaper readership is larger. Our relevance feels greater.

As a young clerk at the *New York Post*, I worked night shifts with Vic Ziegel—one of my favorite reads during my late teen and early adult years—who was helping out with editing on the night desk. This was at the sunset of Muhammad Ali's storied career and after Ziegel had been the *Post*'s star correspondent, trailing after him to Africa, the Philippines, and other distant ports during the height of his fame as the self-proclaimed *greatest* and an anti-war activist. The stories Ziegel passed down to me and the younger generational wannabes those nights were priceless. They made sportswriting sound so exotic, and so consequential, that for the first time in my budding career I was consumed with succeeding at it.

The dawn of the Riley era, starting with the night he led an arena in prayer for Magic Johnson, felt like the beginning of something special in New York. In retrospect, Riley could not have arrived at a more propitious time for me. My hiring at the *Times* had been set to the rollout of a planned expansion of the newspaper's sports pages. Long a stepchild section, situated at the rear of Business or Metro, Sports was getting a makeover, its own daily pullout.

In the tabloid world, sports sell papers, which meant it was always essential to have comprehensive coverage of nighttime events in the morning editions. In order to survive, we had to be fast and meet brutal deadlines. The *Times*, conversely, had traditionally run on less-urgent sports-production cycles, given its obvious priorities of covering Washington and the world. But in the early nineties, *Newsday*, a literate tabloid with bountiful *Los Angeles Times* revenues behind it, was pushing into the city from its home base on Long Island. The *Times* perceived it as a threat, and responded by devoting increased resources to New York City news and sports. Neil Amdur, the sports editor, was given a mandate to quicken the pulse of the report, to compete harder with the tabloids on the New York pro beats. The simultaneous hiring of Filip Bondy and me from the *Daily News* seemed to be a statement of that intention to compete. How lucky for me that the expanded section I was newly working for was now, like our local competitors, seeking a sexy New York story to ride. It turned out to be the Knicks, and the sport I was putatively hired to cover.

In New York, the Yankees were in a down cycle. The Mets were a faded National League power of the eighties. The NFL's Giants were in a post–Bill Parcells depression and the Jets were, as usual, no sight for sore eyes. Hockey was never a game for the masses. That left Riley's upstart Knicks in particular and the NBA in general, both rapidly on the rise—not only locally, but globally.

Not long after the 1992 playoffs ended with the Bulls winning their second straight title, I embarked on a summer journey to chronicle the fortunes of the Olympic Dream Team. It was a tough life I led—a week in San Diego for the team's training camp; another week in Portland, Oregon, for the Americas Olympic qualifying tournament; a few days of final preparation before the Summer Games, dictating stories to the office from the rooftop pool of a Monte Carlo hotel overlooking the Mediterranean Sea; and on to Barcelona, where track stars, gymnasts, and swimmers—normally the marquee attractions of the Summer Olympics—genuflected in the presence of Magic, Larry, and Michael.

As groundbreaking a concept as the Dream Team was—American corporate warriors invading the loosely defined amateur domain—I was more fascinated by the narratives of their overmatched competition, especially those remapped countries in a fast-changing geopolitical landscape. In the wake of the ongoing dissolution of the Soviet Union and the Yugoslavian

Communist strangleholds on neighboring lands, the theme of nationalistic pride was rampant at the basketball venue. Halfway through the tournament, I learned of two players from Latvia who had joined what was called the Unified Team, a hastily arranged and officially flagless team for players who had been part of the Soviet sports machine. In Latvia—which, unlike the former Soviet satellite and basketball-rich Lithuania, hadn't qualified for the Olympics—the two players were denounced as traitors for teaming with a group that reflected their longtime Russian occupiers. The debate over whether athletes with finite time to compete in an Olympics should concern themselves with politics was ideal for the *Times*'s sports sensibilities. The story made the paper's front page—and was the first thing out of Michelle's mouth when I returned home and checked in. "I called everyone and said, 'Harvey's on the front page of the *Times*!'" she said. She also rushed out to a news vendor in Stamford, snapped up a bunch of copies, and mailed them around.

For someone fully entrenched in the world of New York media, being on A-1 of the *Times* was like waking up in the swankiest of Manhattan penthouses—it was thrilling, but I also wondered what the hell I was doing there. Writing about Michael Jordan was one thing. Being on the front page of the *Times* with a story that explored cultural fallout from the breakup of the Soviet Union was many levels above my aspirational dreams. A-1 was also rarefied journalistic real estate that brought heightened scrutiny from the newspaper's most meticulous editors, not to mention readers who considered it academic sport to find a dangling participle or even a misplaced comma in the Gray Lady. I couldn't help but feel like something of an impostor.

From Michelle's vantage point, I had achieved journalism nirvana, but her enthusiasm was less of the gee-whiz variety, more atta-boy cheerleading combined with a career coach's satisfaction of seeing her protégé stretch his limits. I, of course, craved such approval, the affirmation I could not get from my family—not because they didn't care, but because they all lived in a world where *nobody reads that paper.*

If any one story turned out to be most worthy of retelling, of sharing with the next generation à la Vic Ziegel, it was my summer with the Dream Team, with an addendum that helped produce a stunning residual career benefit. It occurred a couple of months after returning from Spain, when I walked into the visitors' locker room at Madison Square Garden before a preseason game between the Knicks and the Utah Jazz and there, alone, sat a shirtless Karl Malone, the All-Star power forward and Dream Team member. I am certain that he did not remember my name, but he surely recognized me as one of the handful of reporters who had been embedded with the greatest team ever assembled in any sport.

I sat down alongside him and said that I, like every other NBA league reporter, was working on a welcome-back Magic Johnson story. (Magic, after enjoying the Olympics so much and having experienced no ill effects to his body, had come home and promptly unretired.) Malone stopped me before I could ask a question. "Look at this, scabs and cuts all over me," he said, pressing a finger to a small pinkish hole on his thigh that was developing into a scab. "I get these things every night, every game. They can't tell you that you're not at risk, and you can't tell me there's one guy in the NBA who hasn't thought about it."

Before the Olympics, there had been some apprehension expressed about competing against Magic, though nothing that lingered. But that was prior to a tournament that no one believed would be much more than a Dream Team promotional showcase, nothing like NBA nightly combat. Malone wasn't finished, far from it. "Just because he came back doesn't mean nothing to me," he said. "I'm no fan, no cheerleader. It may be good for basketball, but you have to look far beyond that. You have a lot of young men who have a long life ahead of them. The Dream Team was a concept everybody loved. But now we're back to reality."

By interview's end, I realized that I had stumbled upon a rare NBA player who was willing to go against the tide of love for Magic and air feelings and fears that others were afraid to admit. My story ran the following Sunday in the *Times*, with several other players and executives—a few anonymously—squeamishly supporting Malone's contention that many players and their families were worried about exposure to HIV-contaminated blood. Magic aborted his comeback the very next day, with my story widely cited around the country and presumably the world.

Reporting and writing that story was challenging and not much fun. For his unflinching honesty, Malone became the face of the unenlightened when he was far from alone at a time when HIV education was not widespread. And Magic was an extraordinarily popular athlete, the gold standard for reporters, who seldom left a session with a notebook unfilled. He was a player I couldn't help but root for. I was conflicted about the story's impact, but back at the *Times*, where my personal feelings were irrelevant, the chain of events caught the attention of the paper's masthead editors—not a bad thing when the sports pages were suddenly more of a priority. Within a year I found myself nominated for a Pulitzer Prize for a wide range of basketball coverage—from a series on a troubled high school team in Brooklyn to the announcement of Jordan's so-called sabbatical from the Chicago Bulls. The same week that Jordan took leave of the Bulls on the eve of the 1993–94 season training camp, I was summoned to the office by Amdur, the sports editor, and offered a chance to write a general sports column. I hadn't yet been at the *Times*—an institution where dues paying was legendary—for three years, and I was being asked to join the Sports of the Times rotation.

The column held a vaunted place at the *Times* and in a media landscape very different from today's. No newspaper was yet online. The popular opinion shows on ESPN—*Pardon the Interruption*, *Around the Horn*—were yet to appear. Even twenty-four-hour sports talk radio was only a developing concept. Opinion—and especially informed opinion—was not readily accessible. Terrific sports columnists were churning out multiple pieces a week at dailies large and small across the country. But only the *Times* had measurable reach outside its own local market. The case could be made that a Sports of the Times column was the industry apex.

It was also, I suppose, why I told Amdur that I needed time to think about the offer and spent the next few days trying to talk myself out of it while wrestling with my father's old refrain: *What do you need it for?* I already had a highly visible gig—a legitimate comfort zone—covering the NBA. I figured Michelle, who had no use for the other major sports, would agree. I couldn't have been more wrong. She was incredulous—as I am all these years later—that I hadn't accepted the column on the spot. She suggested I stop bullshitting myself—it had nothing to do with basketball or a more comfortable life. "If you turn it down, it'll be for one reason and one reason only: fear," she said. "And there's only one reason why you would be afraid—because you think you don't deserve it."

She was right, of course. The *Times* column represented much more than a collection of results, a tabulation of winners and losers. This was where readers—and in this newspaper's case, the highest brows of sports-minded readers—went for informed clarity on the issues. It was one thing to break down the game, profile players on the NBA beat. But the blue-collar kid and college transient in me wasn't quite ready to believe that I could play to this upscale crowd.

"Did you ever think they want you because you *do* sound different than the people they've had?" Michelle said. This was vintage Michelle, my loyal and brutally honest human resource, who recognized the prestige of the Sports of the Times column, who knew it was a destination position—not to mention the home of her favorite sports columnist, George Vecsey. The others were Dave Anderson, a dean of American sports journalism, and Ira Berkow, a renowned storyteller.

How, Michelle wondered, could I possibly pass up an opportunity to join such an esteemed rotation? If I allowed fear to dictate my decision, I would regret it for the rest of my life. "That's a long time—hopefully," I joked. I told her that I would probably take the job but reserved the right to blame her if I was miserable doing it. Fine, she said, if that's what it'd take.

Over the next fifteen years, there were more than a few days when I cringed while trudging into football locker rooms filled with hulking gladiators, endured the Steinbrenner circus under the Yankee Stadium big tent, and furiously wrestled with the social and cultural issues that spilled from real life onto the sports pages. It wasn't always a treat waking up to a flood of nasty email responses from readers, or knee-jerk tweets from socially or politically offended readers in a deeply coarsening culture.

Writing the column was also a job that could be maddeningly all-consuming and life disrupting—inviting disapproving looks from Beth when she and the boys talked to a man whose mind had wandered off to the next column on the work schedule. But regret? Never. The work was challenging, growth inducing, deeply rewarding. Each column had the potential to be an empowering process of self-actualization: *I wrote it, I believe it, I stand by it.* My fifteen years of sharing the Sports of the Times space with Vecsey, Anderson, Berkow, and later Selena Roberts and William C. Rhoden would be the proudest of my journalism career. As she did when I wavered in my decisions to leave the *Post* and the *Daily News*, Michelle had put her own basketball rooting and reading preferences aside and helped steer me right again.

Eight

·　·　·　·　·　·　·　·　·　·　·

Winning and Misery

Michelle didn't watch live games the way other fans did. While friends like Ernestine Miller and Drucie De Vries whooped it up in triumphant Knicks moments—such as they were—with all their courtside neighbors, Michelle sat calmly, stoically, barely shifting in her seat. She never yelled at the refs or the opposing players. She didn't erupt with joy when the Knicks pulled out a close one. The occasional section resident would sidle up to Miller and ask why Michelle was so muted. "She's an observer of the game—she shows interest in her own way," Miller would tell them, herself guessing.

But while she never would change her game demeanor, the 1992–93 season, and specifically the playoffs, provided plenty of opportunity for high drama. Until the night of Game 2 of the Eastern Conference Finals, or actually through that night, all had been proceeding on championship schedule for Pat Riley and his marauding Knicks. They rose to the top of the conference, winning sixty regular-season games, second-best in the league and three more than the Michael Jordan–led Bulls. To further whet their fans' appetite for the playoffs, they took three of four of their head-to-head meetings. They marched through the first two rounds, setting up another showdown with the two-time defending champions in the Eastern Conference Finals. Only this time, the Knicks had home-court advantage, which meant that a seventh game, if necessary, would be played in New York.

"I keep pinching myself," Michelle told me again and again—it was her standard line when the promise of Knicks greatness peeked through the perpetual cloud cover—as that season progressed. It was no dream, though it felt like the continuation of Riley's fantasy life with all of New York along for the ride. These brawny, emboldened Knicks looked formidable holding serve against the Bulls in Game 1 at the Garden. In Game 2, John Starks, a onetime minimum-wage supermarket stock boy, went airborne and dunked like Mike, famously posterizing Jordan and his teammate, Horace Grant, and icing the game for a 2–0 series lead. The Garden joyously erupted. The Bulls looked vulnerable. Better yet, Jordan looked mortal. We soon had answers—or at least educated guesses—as to why.

At halftime of that game, Dave Anderson, my fellow *Times* columnist, strolled my way with a tip: Throughout the first half, he had been listening to a fan behind his seat along the baseline hector Jordan about being in Atlantic City early that morning. This was not exactly shocking information—Jordan's gambling excesses, occasionally with characters of questionable repute, were already a media preoccupation, a cloud hanging over him and the league. But Anderson and I agreed: If he had actually been out in the wee hours on the morning of a playoff game, that was a story we needed to pursue because it spoke to his level of commitment to his team.

Jordan's heckler laughed when I made my way over and introduced myself—as if to say, *What took you so long?*—and proceeded to tell me that he had been in the casino at Bally's Grand Hotel in the early morning hours and had seen Jordan up close and personal. Anderson, a longtime boxing insider who knew his way around Atlantic City casinos, had sources who could confirm the fan's report—and more.

Anderson's column on the morning of May 27 was titled "Jordan's Atlantic City Caper," reporting that Jordan had been in the casino as late as two thirty a.m. and had dropped five thousand dollars playing blackjack in a private room. That was lunch money for him—but not the point. Anderson noted that while Jordan scored thirty-six points in Game 2, only eleven were in the second half. He questioned the sport's preeminent star's "devotion to duty." An accompanying story with my byline—headlined "Bulls Seem to Be Playing Without a Full Deck"—mocked Jordan's card-playing predilection. I quoted Jerry Krause, the Bulls' general manager, who said, "I can't believe Michael would do something like that," but my story also reported that radio stations in Atlantic City and Philadelphia had received calls from additional casino eyewitnesses.

As the series shifted to Chicago, the *Times* coverage was picked up nationwide. A furious Jordan launched a boycott of all media. Back in Stamford, meanwhile, Michelle was convinced that Anderson and I had reset the series' competitive karma. "What the *hell* have you guys done?" she barked.

And she was right. Michelle had good reason to believe that we had poked the wrong bear and doomed the Knicks: Thanks to her work with high-level executives, she was familiar with the alpha-male ego, the leveraged power broker with an inflated sense of competitive entitlement. Jordan, in a nutshell. He weaponized his perceived media persecution against the Knicks and led the Bulls to two series-tying wins. Meanwhile, the *Times*, Anderson, and I were taking a verbal lashing on New York's sports talk radio station—which Michelle listened to religiously in her car and in her kitchen. "If I didn't love you, Harvey, I'd want to kill you," she said when I paid her a visit at her seat before Game 5 tipped off back at the Garden.

But in an industry with an ever-evolving narrative in conjunction with the almighty short attention span, there was always another day, another game, the next winner to extol—and, in this case, loser to deride. In what now was a best-of-three series, Anderson and I would not remain the most hated men in town for much longer.

Fast-forward roughly a quarter century—Michelle relaxing in the Garden's Delta Sky360 Club, where she was de facto royalty; on game nights two seats at the bar were unofficially but routinely reserved for her and whoever happened to be using her second ticket. On this night, it was Gary Shillet, her colleague from the School of Visual Arts. Shillet, the school's chief financial officer, was enjoying a light dinner and drinks with

Michelle when she noticed a familiarly tall, slender man strid-
ing their way. Without pause, she turned to Shillet and lowered
her voice.

"Charles Smith is coming over to say hello," she told him.
"He's a friend of mine—so don't you dare say anything about
those missed layups!"

Like any adult Knicks fan who hadn't gone to sleep for twenty
years just before the night of June 2, 1993, Shillet well remembered the "layups" that were actually recorded as three blocked
shots and one strip of the ball—aborted attempts destined to live
forever in Knicks lore for all the wrong reasons. They comprised
the sad conclusion to Game 5 of the 1993 Eastern Conference Finals, often referred to as just that—Game 5. More cruelly, it was
also sometimes remembered as the Charles Smith Game.

Michelle was proud and protective of her relationships with
Smith, Walt Frazier, and other former Knicks who made the club
rounds but on occasion hunkered down to chat or dine with her.
She felt compelled to warn Shillet, among other companions,
because experience had shown her that many fans—desensitized
by a little booze or a belief that highly compensated professional
athletes were not necessarily deserving of common courtesy—
couldn't help themselves. Especially in the case of Smith.

It wasn't necessarily the regulars, those accustomed to seeing
Smith around. It was more the Wall Street brokers who'd get
their company tickets and club privileges once or twice a year
and hit the complimentary bar hard. *Oh, there's Charles Smith, let's
go over and give him shit.* Michelle hated these intrusions and was
determined to make sure it wouldn't happen with anyone in her
company. Astonishing to me was her ability, even in what she

presumed to be the earliest stages of the dreaded dementia, to correctly recall the exact number—fifteen—of free throws the Knicks had missed in the pivotal Game 5, leading to a Game 6 elimination in Chicago. She had long reached the conclusion that the defeat had been, above all, a collective act of self-sabotage. A quarter century later, during one of our 2017–18 season dinners, she would preach to me—by then the choir—that Smith had been a convenient scapegoat, a face to plaster onto collaborative failure. Emboldened by a glass or two of red wine, she grew more intense, even indignant, on the subject of Game 5 and its ongoing aftermath.

"It was the free throws they missed," she said.

Pause.

"And of course you and Dave Anderson had to piss off Michael in the first place."

I laughed, happy to see that her memory—at least on Knicks matters of the highest import—was just fine.

All was not lost—at least not all championship hope—after Riley's Knicks failed to reach the NBA Finals in 1993. Just when it appeared that they would never be able to get past the Bulls as long as Jordan was around, he did them an astonishing favor by not being around.

Weeks before the 1993–94 season tipped off, he took what turned out to be a seventeen-month sabbatical from the Bulls, positioning the Knicks, if only by default, as the clear favorites in the Eastern Conference. By late spring, deep into the playoffs, they were right where they wanted to be—though barely. They survived a seven-game series with the Jordan-less Bulls, thanks to a charitable foul call that kept them from a repeat blown Game 5 at home. They narrowly withstood the dazzling shooting theatrics of Reggie Miller—inspired by the courtside heckling of Spike Lee, whose look-at-me antics infuriated Michelle—to hold off the Indiana Pacers and advance to the league Finals against the Houston Rockets.

The Knicks were on what looked to be a magical run and Michelle, in her subdued way, was exultant. If anyone had ever doubted her sincerity, her passion, they only had to check her travel itinerary during that playoff season. With her business thriving and her work commitments made well in advance, she juggled frantically the many demands on her time to ensure that she would be courtside when the games tipped off. In her 1994 Christmas letter, she offered insight into the logistical chaos her passion for the team required:

> *The playoffs are a different breed. They cannot be scheduled until mere days ahead due to the outcome of the final standings & the preceding series, home-court advantage, NBC, TNT & TBS. I made them all, minus one. A Herculean effort. One trip, racing back from California to make an Eastern Conference final (Game 2 vs. the Pacers was booked on four different airlines from two different cities into two different states and three different airports). Some direct flights, some connecting flights. All to ensure that bad weather, missing hub*

connections and/or mechanical aircraft problems would
not keep me from making it to Madison Square Garden by
game time.

For those riveting spring months in 1994, going to work was a privilege, an invitation to chronicle history, punctuate the Riley saga I was convinced I'd be retelling—like Ziegel with his old Ali tour stories—deep into old age. The Knicks just needed to win four more games.

Like the Knicks, Houston was built around a star center, Hakeem Olajuwon. Neither team had an established second star. The series was predictably tight, deadlocked at 2–2 going into Game 5 on a sweltering night, June 17, in New York. It was a game Ewing dominated, furiously swatting away shots, outplaying Olajuwon, finally living up to the early Bill Russell defensive comparisons and leaving the Knicks one victory shy of a championship. But just their luck, and in keeping with the star-crossed nature of Ewing's career, most of the country and even a fair number of New Yorkers hardly noticed or cared.

That night, the most consequential shot was the one O. J. Simpson—holding a .357 Magnum to his head in the backseat of white Ford Bronco—never took. But O. J. on the loose, his friend Al Cowlings at the wheel and the California Highway Patrol in full pursuit, made for gripping viewing. It was reality TV before its time, and who could resist a chase that was far more compelling than the Knicks' then-twenty-one-year quest for a crown?

At courtside, the white Bronco initially appeared on the NBC telecast in a box inset at the top of the television screen sitting on the press table during the second quarter. Then came a split-screen and finally a complete cutaway from the Garden, even as the NBA commissioner, David Stern, pleaded at courtside with NBC's Dick Ebersol to stay the basketball course.

Near the Knicks bench, on a small press row set, we kept one eye on the Bronco motoring down the 405 while fans scrambled around the arena in search of a screen. Michelle, of course, didn't have far to go. During stoppages in the action, she practically set her chin on my right shoulder for her O. J. updates. "You paid *how* much to watch this while your team is playing for the championship?" I asked. She laughed at the absurdity of it all, real life intruding on her world of fun and games. Meanwhile, I was facing another frightful deadline, trying to make sense of the madness while the Garden fans chanted, "One more, one more."

Game 5 wound up as the lowest-rated Finals game in fifteen years. The O. J. chase outdrew that year's Super Bowl. But by night's end, he was in handcuffs. The Knicks didn't have time to worry about ratings, or O. J. Game 6 was less than forty-eight hours away. They would soon be on their way back to Houston, and within hours I would be heading there, too. At the final buzzer, I hit the send key on my deadline column and rose from my seat for another fire drill of interviewing and late-night updating, only to be met by Michelle.

"When are you leaving?" she said.

"For where?"

"For Houston, where else?"

"Tomorrow afternoon," I said. "Why?"

"Because I've been sitting here for twenty fucking years and I'll be damned if they're going to win the championship without me being there."

You would have thought that a four-plus-hour flight would be the last thing a woman who spent as much time traveling for work as Michelle did would have volunteered for. I suspected she was overreacting to the moment and would soon go home and remember how comfortable her living room couch was. But the next morning, she called to say that she had indeed tapped a Garden source and secured tickets to Game 6 and, if necessary, Game 7. She had rearranged her work schedule and booked her flight. She just needed to know which hotel I would be staying at, and she would be set. Like Spike Lee—only without cameras recording her presence—she was going to Houston, going the distance, deep in the heart of Texas.

The following night, the Knicks played valiantly and had a fine chance to end the series in a tensely fought Game 6. Olajuwon, however, switched off on Ewing to deflect John Starks's three-point shot at the buzzer—a play originally designed for Ewing, broken by Starks—and the Rockets won by two. That meant three long days to wait for Game 7 in Houston, a sprawling, oppressively hot and humid city. Sunlight reflected off glass towers everywhere, creating the feeling of being on the set of some futuristic climate disaster flick. Michelle hated the weather, hated Houston, and spent most of her time between games in the air-conditioned hotel, visiting the gym, and making calls. We had dinner out one night, and on one afternoon I coaxed her into visiting a new museum at NASA's Johnson Space Center. A photo of us was taken in the gift shop—I don't remember why or by whom, only that I loved how it wound up hanging in the workout room of Michelle's condo, near her framed Knicks jersey.

At lunch that day, she asked if I thought the Knicks would win Game 7. Sportswriter predictions are seldom worth the paper or pixels with which they are printed, but seldom did we miss an opportunity to make one. I said I was tempted to bet on the mystique of Riley over the forbidding road-team odds. "I don't know," she said. "I think maybe they had their chance the other night and they didn't do it."

I told her she was being a fatalist—normally my thing—but in retrospect, my gut instinct was based more on wishful thinking. We had already come as far as we possibly could in the playoffs, leaving no bonus time off with the family left in the season to root for. I found myself wanting the Knicks to win, pulling for the story to play out to its most fanciful—or fairy-tale—ending. I had also grown to admire Ewing's quiet determination and wished for him to get his ring. On top of it all, I wanted Michelle to be rewarded for her commitment, her effort. Was one measly title too much to ask?

Unfortunately, Ewing was outplayed by Olajuwon in Game 7 while Starks set himself up for the Charles Smith treatment by missing sixteen of eighteen shots, in the process sentencing Riley to an eternity of second-guessing for not benching his mercurial guard. In Riley's defense, Starks had been a money player—arguably *the* money player—all season. Right to the last misfire, the coach was convinced that Starks was going to make a big one. Never had I ever seen *any* coach so visibly distraught in the immediate aftermath of defeat—though apparently more for Ewing than for himself. Riley's voice choked with sadness as he said, "It's a deep, deep hurt for him right now—there's not anybody in the room who doesn't know how much he wants it."

It was classic Riley—seizing the moment, stretching the drama to melodrama, rendering all of us putty in his soft hands. Of course, in doing what we do, we overdo. That has always been the lore and lure of sports, applying life-and-death consequences to what amounts to a few hours of athletic entertainment. The reality was that nobody had died. Ewing and the Knicks would be back within three months to play on, handsomely compensated in the process. Still, Riley had a knack for making a championship chase feel like the pursuit of world peace. Those Knicks were cloned from the competitive DNA of the man whose working mantra had long been: "There is winning . . . and there is misery."

Back at the hotel, where Michelle had waited up for me to share a late-night drink and rehash the game, she wasn't buying the Riley dogma, which he had repeated. "I don't think he means it literally," she said. "It's part of his genius, the sales pitch to his team, the way he gets them to play every night like their lives depend on it."

Nor did she sound too distressed over losing. Apparently, she wasn't. "Look at how far they got," she said. "I can't be upset. They did their best." Indeed, most nights that season and throughout the Riley years, the Knicks had "shown up"—another standard Michelle application of acceptable effort from her team. It meant they had, win or lose, played hard, lived up to their end of the bargain. That was all she—or any reasonable fan—could ask.

The next morning, on the plane ride back to Newark, I thought about Michelle's positivity, her contention that there was, and had to be, an emotional space to stake out between winning and misery. It actually surprised me how quickly she could be so damned reasonable after such a wrenching defeat. In time, I realized it was because Michelle, at heart, was more realist than romantic. Life had already been too challenging, too unpredictable, for her to expect endings scripted by Disney. As long as you tried, *really* tried, you could rationalize failure as part of the deal. And so I came to better understand what it was Michelle most wanted from the Knicks and, in a larger sense, her commitment to them. More than the Garden's social benefits, more than any championship parade, her love of the journey was what defined her as a fan. By virtue of showing up, night after night, season after season, she didn't have to make a scene, or become unhinged in moments of triumph or torment, to prove how much she appreciated the life that she had.

One year later, in May 1995, with Jordan back with the Bulls and a young Shaquille O'Neal dominating opponents in Orlando, speculation mounted that the Knicks' best chance at a championship had passed and that their partnership with Pat Riley was in serious jeopardy. The insiders knew he was restless and believed to be on the way out as the Knicks fell into a 3–1 hole during a second-round series with Miller and the Pacers. On Wednesday, May 17, 1995, they were trailing by a point with 5.9 seconds remaining in another tense Game 5. On deadline again,

I looked around the lower bowl of the arena and began frantically typing:

> Fans stood in disbelief, drained and depressed. The Knicks, down a point, down to their last shot, huddled up. Around the arena, people cupped their hands over their mouths. Companions had their arms draped over each other's shoulders. Someone opposite the Pacers' bench decided to get a jump on next season and raised a sign that read: "Riley, please stay."

Play resumed. The ball went to Ewing, who spun into the lane and dropped in a shot to save the Knicks—though only for a few more days before a heartbreaking defeat in Game 7 that ended with Ewing misfiring pretty much the same shot in the exact same place. But before his Game 5 basket prolonged the series, in the year of the twenty-fifth anniversary of the franchise's first championship, it also occurred to me that the Garden fans had come to the realization that Riley's title-less team had carved its own indelible identity, staked out its own sacred space. It had, in effect, come around to Michelle's way of thinking after the "misery" of falling short in Houston. For those too young to remember the days of Reed and Frazier and Monroe, *these* would ultimately be remembered as a special time in their own right. Thus, my column continued:

> Riley has said there are only two possible endings to a season, "winning and misery." If he honestly believes that, that's his problem. The notion that a Knicks

defeat tomorrow night in Indianapolis renders the last four seasons meaningless is absurd, the ranting of sports talk radio.

Of course, the genesis of that night's column—renouncing Riley's rhetoric—had occurred a year earlier over that late-night drink at the Houston hotel bar. With many personal triumphs and challenges ahead, I had a long way to go before I could embrace Michelle's more dispassionate and contextualized approach to life. But she was making her unmistakable mark on me. She was more than a column collaborator. She was, in many ways, its conscience.

Nine

Dolan and the
Death of Hope

To say that Michelle could hold her own when matched in the corporate arena with powerful men was an understatement. She had her own thriving business to prove it. By her midsixties she had conducted countless management seminars and had become a flourishing outsourced fixer, empowered by major companies to chasten and reorient the power brokers who, for any number of reasons, had created toxic work environments.

It wasn't surprising, or uncommon, that some of these men responded to her workplace inquisitions and analyses with deflection, denial, or outright indignation. But by this point of her life, Michelle's skin was toughened by personal *and* professional experience. Absorbing the hostility was just part of her deal, the challenge of convincing Mr. Corporate America that She—a woman with clout—was actually trying to help him.

She thought she had seen and heard it all—until James Dolan was elevated to the chairmanship of Madison Square Garden around the turn of the century and became the operating controller of her beloved Knicks. Over the next two decades, this scion of the Cablevision television empire would become the most confounding organizational strongman she had ever laid eyes on, one seemingly bent on defeating himself.

In his younger days, Dolan, a singer and guitar player, had pursued a career in music without much success before going into the family business. Handed the reins to the Garden by his father, Charles, he took his place among other alpha-male sports owners in New York—except he wasn't bombastically entertaining like the Yankees' George Steinbrenner or buttoned-down collegial like the Giants' John Mara. As a public figure, Dolan was a virtual nonentity. He shunned the media. He seemed to want nothing to do with the fan bases of the Knicks and the Garden's co-tenant, the Rangers hockey team. On nights when he showed up to watch his Knicks, he interacted with almost no one, including even his small circle of sycophants.

Dolan's seat in the renovated Garden—front row, baseline— was a long bounce pass from Michelle's, providing her an angled window into his courtside lair, where he typically was flanked by company aides or a freeloading friend. She inevitably would fix her gaze upon him, try to apply corporate and common sense to an uncommonly dour man. *Why won't he put on a happier face?* she wondered. Why did he slump in his seat, arms folded across his chest, like some bored, petulant child? He surely had the worst public posture she had ever seen from a corporate executive.

"Anybody would look at him and come to the conclusion that he just didn't give a shit," she said.

Deciphering Dolan quickly became a required but formidable

exercise for the city's basketball media and fans. For Michelle—who, after all, was trained for the job—going to a game and watching Dolan in action was not all that unlike a day at the office. She would sometimes ask herself what conclusions she might have drawn had she been assigned to "fix" one of the most disliked owners in the history of New York sports. But in a brochure for the consulting company she launched in 1986—the Training Advantage, LTD—and long before she had ever heard of Dolan, she had happened to author an effective primer for the problems he eventually would pose for the Knicks:

> Stars: Every organization has them. They're financial whizzes. Technical geniuses. Sales powerhouses. Market wizards. They're also tireless, indispensable and—unfortunately—occasionally intolerable.
>
> They don't listen; they dominate. They don't reason; they rage. They don't build up; they tear down. Their intellectual abilities have gotten them—and your organization—quite far. But without change of some kind, stars like these don't merely shine. They burn. Their caustic behavior damages working relationships, harming others as well as themselves.

To be clear, few, if any, people thought of Dolan as a "financial whiz" or "technical genius." A better argument could be made that the majority of the success enjoyed by the Garden as an entertainment center was based on location, in the heart of Manhattan. Also not to be overlooked was the almost $50 million in annual tax rebates granted by the city long before Dolan's ascension.

In 2019, *Forbes* appraised the Knicks' value at $4 billion, equal to that of the Yankees, and second in North America only to the NFL's Dallas Cowboys. Even in an era of franchise inflation, it was a staggering figure. And yet, around the same time, a group of shareholders from the Garden's publicly traded company claimed in a lawsuit that Dolan was dramatically overpaying himself while spending too much time as front man for a marginal blues band benefiting from the arena's showbiz connections.

Under Dolan's stewardship, the Knicks have experienced nearly two decades of mostly horrendous basketball, with a revolving cast of forgettable and, in some cases, detestable characters. The notoriously combative owner, among his other greatest behavioral fits, occasionally tore into complaining fans as "assholes" and "drunks," while himself a recovering alcoholic. Bound to say or do something wantonly damaging to the Knicks brand, creating a news-breaking firestorm while doing so, Dolan became a godsend for those of us churning out sports columns. But no critic cut to the bone quite like Selena Roberts, my former Sports of the Times colleague, who in October 2007 authored a scathing piece titled "The Garden Needs a Warning Label":

> As the legend goes, it was years ago, aboard a sleek family yacht, when Charles F. Dolan asked his executive crewmates an earnest question: "What about Jim?"
>
> His son needed an occupation. Something to divert his rock-star ambitions. Something to focus him. So he decided to give James L. Dolan what amounted to a skate key to Madison Square Garden, a business

irrelevant to Cable Daddy's vast bottom line, a play-ground where his son could do no harm.

Except Jim turned his toy into a weapon. Inside the Garden, "Got Hurt?" has become the slogan for vulnerable staffers. For years, he had wounded careers and savaged dissenters while assembling a cult of personality where only his sycophants survive amid a game of Jim-nastics.

Roberts's killer column was one piece of a savage media beating that Dolan was taking in New York and beyond. A sexual harassment civil trial brought against the Garden and Isiah Thomas, then the Knicks' president and general manager, by a fired marketing director named Anucha Browne Sanders had exposed a side to the team's operations far worse than mere incompetence.

Dolan didn't help matters, or his own image, in a deposition video that found its way to the viewing public. He wore a collarless black shirt, his body slumped and his head bobbing as if he might nod off. Michelle couldn't believe what she was seeing. "He showed up not dressed in a suit, like the whole thing wasn't worth his time," she told me. "Dress the part and sit up straight, you idiot!"

Dolan explained his reasoning for not settling out of court by claiming, "The fighter came out in me." Michelle read something beyond defiance, not only because Dolan stood by Thomas for a time, but because even after firing him for poor team performance, he brought him back to the Garden—as president of the group's WNBA franchise! He actually seemed to enjoy "spitting in people's eyes." But not surprisingly, his pricey defense in the Browne Sanders case went down like a punch-drunk heavyweight, costing Dolan and his organization $11.5 million in damages, plus lawyers' fees. A negotiated settlement would surely have amounted to a fraction of that amount.

In the process, Dolan allowed the allegations of misogyny against Thomas to be revealed and painstakingly repeated, insult by profane insult. Michelle—along with anyone who understood how corporate America operated—was astonished that Dolan had let the case go that far and failed to protect the reputation of his company, if not Thomas, his supposed friend. The inflated compensation package doubled as a microcosm of the paradox Dolan presented to Knicks fans. Upon assuming the Garden chairmanship, he reportedly told Dave Checketts, still the building's president, "Don't you ever lose a player over money," and he backed that up by spending big bucks on his team, overpaying when necessary. It provided him a reasonable defense against his many critics. He really did want to win.

In his defense, Dolan did rise to controlling power at an unfortunate time, just as the Patrick Ewing era was winding down. The post-Riley years had been surprisingly fertile under the coaching guidance of Jeff Van Gundy, a brash but likable Riley disciple who was given the job at the startling age of thirty-four. Standing all of five feet nine, he became an immediate favorite of Michelle's, who no longer had her courtside view obstructed by someone over six feet tall.

Riley, meanwhile, went to Miami and built another team in his combative image. As it turned out, every NBA postseason between 1997 and 2000 featured a bitter playoff showdown between the Knicks and the Heat, Van Gundy and Riley, Ewing and Alonzo Mourning, his fellow Georgetown alum. So accustomed did Michelle become to seeing Riley on the opposing bench, it was as if he had never left the Garden but had only switched roles, the hero wrestler turned heel. Better yet, Van Gundy's Knicks won three of the four showdowns, a brawling brand of basketball that was akin to awaiting a wreck at the Daytona 500. Although neither team won a title, the Knicks, after barely slipping into the 1999 playoffs and upsetting the Heat in the first round, did reach the Finals, where, without an injured Ewing, they went down in five games to the San Antonio Spurs.

By 2000, Ewing was aging and cranky, feeling unappreciated by an organization that was planning for life without him. He requested a trade and was shipped to Seattle. Within months, the savvy Checketts was gone from the Garden's executive suite. Not long after, Van Gundy, the self-deprecating everyman who had replaced Riley, the image-conscious *perfect* man, vacated the coaching sidelines. By that time, it was clear that something ominous was happening at the Garden, behind the scenes. Reports from disgruntled insiders and those who had departed spoke of a reign of organizational terror ignited by an imperious and volatile Dolan. Morale around the arena began to reflect his leadership—on the court and off.

It was no place for an earnest, honest public relations person. Lori Hamamoto moved on from her coveted PR director's job, another Michelle favorite gone. Other Garden employees she knew who stayed suddenly began excusing themselves after a greeting. Reports of more-hostile media policies soon surfaced. Michelle could almost smell the fear inside the arena, a familiar

The aspiring sports journalist apprenticing at the *Staten Island Advance* in the early seventies, taking it easy between fielding local results by phone.

After graduating from Saint Mary's College in South Bend, Indiana, a youthful Michelle returned to her home state and the University of Connecticut to add a teaching degree.

Michelle with her five young children, born within less than a decade, striking an idyllic pose that belies turbulence at home.

During the celebrated Patrick Ewing era of the nineties, the Knicks could always count on Michelle (*visible between John Starks and Greg Anthony*) to stand tall behind them and, on occasion, to earn some promotional back-page fan cred in the process.

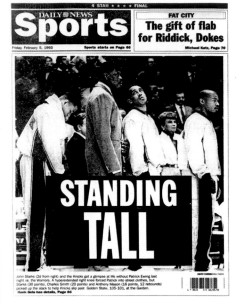

Michelle and her friend Drucie De Vries had their view of the court partially obstructed by the striking visage of Pat Riley, but had less trouble seeing over the shorter, less coiffed Jeff Van Gundy (*left*) after he became head coach.

Despite making frequent use of her lucky orange playoff towel from the late nineties, Michelle (*center*) had her twenty-first-century championship hopes for the Mike D'Antoni–coached Knicks forever dashed by the James Dolan–inspired acquisition of the volume-shooting Carmelo Anthony (*lower right*).

Oblivious to all around her, Michelle preps for a
game by reading a column in the *New York Times*
sports section—hopefully mine—as if it were
a detailed scouting report.

Through the decades, Michelle cultivated an authoritative courtside
presence. Here, she points out something that requires the attention of
a Knicks trainer, Tim Walsh.

Hanging with Michelle at her front-row seat, in my early days on the beat for the *New York Post*. I don't remember whom she was talking to outside the frame, but she was seldom without an opinion to deliver as she held court behind the Knicks bench.

For many of my years covering the Knicks, the press-row seat was steps away from Michelle's, allowing me more time to make a new friend and cultivate a well-placed source.

Inside the Madison Square Garden club for elite ticketholders, Michelle was a celebrity who attracted others to her pregame table, including, on occasion, the great Walt Frazier.

Lori Hamamoto (*left*) grew close to Michelle while working as the Knicks' director of media relations. Charles Oakley (*center*), the team's beloved lunch-pail enforcer in the nineties, told me he considered Michelle "the Oak Man of Knicks fans" for how she showed up every night, through thick and thin.

With the Knicks one win from the 1993–94 championship, Michelle dropped everything and flew to Houston to watch the Knicks lose Games 6 and 7. Between games, we visited the NASA Johnson Space Center and this photo, taken in the gift shop, paid tribute to our friendship in the workout room of her condo.

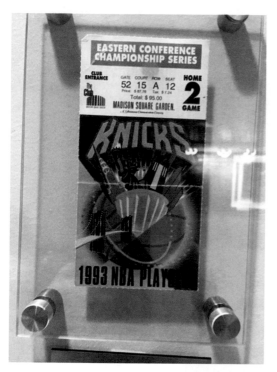

Michelle's ninety-five dollar playoff ticket for the 1993 Eastern Conference Final game—in which John Starks famously dunked on Michael Jordan and the Chicago Bulls—was put on permanent display at the renovated Madison Square Garden, with an accompanying plaque inscribed with her name.

Michelle was a hopeless hoarder of basketball-related memorabilia, including her personal Knicks framed jersey.

The Knicks paid tribute to the absent Michelle on opening night of the 2018–19 season by placing a bouquet of flowers on the seat where her many friends counted on finding her night after night over four-plus decades.

sign of corporate disorder. When the good people left, something had to be wrong at the top.

Many times, she had walked into a large company setting operating in such a poisonous climate, having been hired to trace its origins. Treated with suspicion at best and outright contempt at worst, she would conduct her introductory interview with the person on the hot seat before requesting permission to speak with members of the staff. The process demanded Michelle's gaining the confidence of the employees in order to present a thorough report that would convince the executive to take a long hard look in the mirror.

Dolan, no doubt, would have been a unique challenge. He didn't seem to listen to anyone. Colleagues at the Garden had tried to warn him against letting the Thomas–Browne Sanders case go to trial, to no avail. There was little doubt in Michelle's mind how Dolan would have reacted to someone like her. Nor did she have to stretch her imagination to build a picture of what it was like to work for Dolan, or what his employees would have confided to her if offered anonymity.

But her experience had also told her to view any executive she worked with as complex, not incorrigible. She recognized that there was some kind of positive side to Dolan, expressed via philanthropic interests, especially through a foundation he had established to fight against pancreatic cancer, which had taken the life of a longtime Dolan family ally. He was said to be deeply loyal to some employees. Michelle also believed that his efforts to get and remain sober spoke of an inner strength and possible determination to be a responsible father.

As a student of not only the game but also the business of

basketball, though, Michelle was inclined to look around the league at other owners—and found hers wanting. No one could ignore Dallas's Mark Cuban, to name one example. While Michelle found Cuban's insatiable hunger for attention to be obnoxious at times, his demonstrative fanboy enthusiasm for his team had clearly created a positive environment for players and coaches.

While Cuban thrived on being out front, eager to engage players, fans, and reporters, Dolan was woefully miscast for an owner's social and public obligations. Cuban was a self-made man. Born on third base, Dolan struck Michelle as "probably an angry kid who didn't have much self-esteem, who really wanted to rebel with his music, tell the world that he was pissed off with everything—his father, the pressure to be successful, all of it."

Yet the body language of Dolan the musician intrigued her. He looked different when she watched video clips of him onstage with his band, JD and the Straight Shot, his vibe antithetical to the gloomy, defiant demeanor in his courtside seat. Dolan's day job came with expectations related to his father and his standing in the family. Rocking a fedora, behind a guitar, he looked more comfortable playing with the band than he appeared in the owner's seat—more alive, at peace with the world and himself.

"He may own the Knicks but doesn't seem to know how to make people like him in that role," Michelle said. This all sounded plausible to me. I asked her, half-jokingly, if I could steal her analysis for a column.

While the common fan and media refrain was for Dolan to sell the Knicks, Michelle considered such hopes to be wishful at best, even when the occasional rumor surfaced that he was considering cashing out. Unless there was a full-blown share-holder revolt, Dolan was like many of the executive "stars" Michelle had been hired to help salvage—not to make disappear. Her fantasy was to tackle Dolan as one last project, one long-shot attempt to convince him he had the ability to "make people feel better about the team and about what they were buying."

Dolan habitually did the opposite, to embarrassing extremes, most pitifully confronting fans when they really couldn't be blamed for heckling him, given the Knicks' results during his reign. Noting that Dolan was known for using prepared notes during rare interviews, Michelle wished she could hand him a set of cue cards for different social settings. One, written for the typical disaffected fan, would read: *Stick with us; we're going to give you a winner [big smile and extended hand!].*

She had even entertained the thought of going to David Stern when he was still commissioner, volunteering her services to help Dolan lower the paranoia levels around his arena. Wasn't it in the league's marketing interests to allow reporters less-managed access to players? Would it kill Dolan to occasionally crack a joke or a smile in their presence?

During one of our dinners in the 2017–18 season, Michelle asked if Dolan had ever bothered to say hello to any of the reporters and columnists who were regularly around the team. In my case, there was never so much as a nod, and forget about matching names and faces at one of the many press conferences he threw to introduce the next Knicks executive or coach. In sharp contrast, I told her of the time Jerry Buss, the Lakers' owner, invited the Knicks beat writers into his limousine after a game in Los Angeles, and then left it at our disposal, along with a few of his female friends, for the rest of the night. Granted, that was hedonism, L.A.-style.

With Dolan, we were lucky we didn't get run over. That nearly happened to me in May 2013, when he and his entourage bolted from their seats as the final seconds of a second-round playoff series and fifty-four-win season ticked away against the Pacers in Indianapolis. Racing to the media workroom, I spotted the group at a distance in the corridor, heading my way, Dolan out front. Here was an opportunity to get a quote for my column from the big man himself. Dolan, head down, rushed by, never looked up. Had I been directly in his path with a referee watching, he would have run through me for an offensive foul.

My column the next day made sure to mention that Dolan had "run out" on a rare fine Knicks season without bothering to visit the locker room to offer salutations. A tad spiteful? Perhaps. Inaccurate? Well, no. But while Dolan couldn't be bothered to do the bare minimum to engage or acknowledge reporters, he wasn't above complaining about what was written via his hired help. In the case of the hasty departure from Indy, I was predictably called and told by his PR servant that Dolan and company had only left the arena early to catch a flight back to New York for a hockey playoff game the next night.

"Wait," Michelle cut me off before I could deliver the punch line to this joke of an excuse. "Don't they travel by private jet?"

"Exactly," I said.

Dolan through the years made a series of grand promises to various executives, offering full operational autonomy—which arguably was an impossibility given the financial stakes of the contemporary sports industry. As with all owners, Michelle recognized that Dolan had a right to occasionally weigh in or intervene in some situations. But the question she always wished she could pose to him was why he would want to. What emotional need had his involvement with the Knicks fulfilled? How had it made him a more successful—and happier—man? These were the hard questions she had once posed to the Dolans of corporate America, trying to make them understand that change and growth could transpire only with honest reflection.

Only with that, Michelle believed, could the Knicks restore the exuberance of the nineties, much less the eminence of the seventies. But she also knew that whatever Dolan might do to make things better for his team, it was too late for her to reap any benefits. Because in one of his most infamous and self-defeating cases of meddling, he had succeeded only in making a competitive mockery of her final courtside seasons.

In her company brochures, Michelle liked to use quotes from historical figures to support her strategies, including one from Horace Mann, the nineteenth-century public-education reformer and politician: "If any man seeks for greatness, let him forget greatness and ask for truth, and he will find both."

But as Michelle had written in her company brochure long before Dolan's rise at MSG, men like him didn't listen, they dominated. They didn't reason, they raged. They didn't build up, they tore down. Or at least they went for the most expedient form of construction that had little chance of adhering to championship code. Never was this more glaring than during Donnie Walsh's time at Madison Square Garden.

A highly respected veteran basketball executive hired in 2008 as the Knicks' new team president to clean up the toxicity of Isiah Thomas's five-year run as president and coach, Walsh left the security and relative tranquility of the Indiana Pacers for the opportunity to grow a contender in his native New York. He signed on only after Dolan promised a pledge of noninterference. The arrangement lasted until it no longer suited Dolan's business agenda.

While he was in charge, Walsh hired Mike D'Antoni, an innovative coach who was far ahead of the sport's evolutionary curve. He structured the Knicks' payroll to create a variety of personnel options, in case the most obvious but improbable strategy—luring LeBron James to New York as a free agent in the summer of 2010— failed to materialize. Still in the formative stages of the master plan, Walsh assembled a young, entertaining team by the 2010–11 season, revolving around Amar'e Stoudemire, the free-agent consolation prize he had reeled in when James signed with Miami. Michelle fell hard for that team's competitive spirit and D'Antoni's entertaining, fast-tempo offense—a far cry from the nineties Knicks' savage scrums with Miami.

There was a thrilling night in mid-December 2011 when the Boston Celtics came to the Garden with a 19–4 record and were fortunate to escape with a riveting two-point victory. Two weeks later, San Antonio hit town with a 29–4 mark only to lose, the Knicks piling up 128 points. Michelle was so sure her Knicks were finally on the right track that she dug out a souvenir playoff towel from the nineties and took to draping it across her shoulder at courtside. On the bench, Stoudemire wore a similar orange towel with blue trim for sponsorship considerations. Michelle wore hers in support of Stoudemire—whom she admired for having the guts to tackle New York's pressurized environment—and also as a symbol of hope for better days ahead, like the nineties days of yore.

The city's basketball cognoscenti—myself included—shared her optimism. Walsh still had salary cap flexibility. He had refused to part with future draft picks, as past Knicks regimes had a nasty habit of doing, only to be haunted by their impatience. In other words, Walsh's plan was well conceived. But Dolan had one of his own and it was only marginally related to the proper construction of a basketball team.

That same year, Cablevision had spun off the Garden, its teams, and its cable television network into a publicly traded company. Dolan had also embarked on a three-year, billion-dollar overhaul of the arena, and was planning to help pay for it with a massive increase in premium seating for the following season. Despite the positive reviews of Walsh's foundational work, Dolan wasn't all that impressed. Walsh, after all, hadn't landed James, the marquee prize. Stoudemire wasn't the big-enough brand name Dolan apparently believed he needed to present to fans before their inflated season-ticket packages arrived in their mailboxes that spring. And Stoudemire, as many other potential suitors had feared, had proved to be injury prone, a more legitimate strike against Walsh.

Dolan thus set his sights on Carmelo Anthony, the high-scoring star who was playing in the final season of his contract and wanted out of Denver and into his native New York. The problem was that the New Jersey Nets, heading to Brooklyn under the ownership of the massively wealthy Russian oligarch

Mikhail Prokhorov, were also bidding for Anthony. Denver's front office smartly played the two teams against each other, demanding a ransom of assets for a player who would be a free agent within months that summer. Walsh, who wasn't opposed to acquiring Anthony, an immensely skilled but ball-hogging shotmaker with an aversion to hustling on defense, begged Dolan not to overreact. Dolan didn't listen. As the trade deadline approached and Denver ramped up the pressure, he ordered Walsh to surrender a trove of players and draft picks.

When the deal was finalized on February 21, 2011, the Knicks were two games over .500—and that was exactly how they finished the regular season. They were swept in the first round of the playoffs by Boston. There were factors beyond Anthony's obvious weaknesses as a so-called franchise player—Stoudemire's injuries, for one—but that brief introductory period was a preview of the Anthony era: overhyped and underperforming.

It was all Michelle had to see to know that the Knicks had done it to her again, circumvented due diligence, opted for the sexy acquisition—the wrong one, it turned out—in a league trending toward its biggest names wanting to share the ball and the burden on superteams. Defenders of Anthony argued that the Knicks never provided him a companion star, that they had failed him in the same way they had failed Patrick Ewing. Anthony's detractors, of which I was one, argued that his original sin—forcing the Knicks to surrender the precious assets that might have reeled in a James Harden or a Chris Paul in a trade instead of waiting a few months to sign as a free agent—had sunk his new franchise.

Worse, Anthony's intransigence soon cost the Knicks D'Antoni, who quit when Dolan wouldn't support him in a war of wills with the team's supposed franchise player. Empowered by the owner, Anthony later assisted in snuffing out "Linsanity," the brief Jeremy Lin phenomenon in 2012, when Lin, a little-known Chinese-American point guard out of Harvard, became an instant sensation over a three-week period while Anthony was sitting out with an injury. Lin became the pride of Ivy Leaguers and, more profoundly, Asians everywhere, especially after dominating Kobe Bryant and the Los Angeles Lakers in one eye-opening, thirty-eight-point Friday night explosion at the Garden.

There was no question that Lin had taken the league by surprise, and opponents would soon prepare for him better. But upon returning from his injury, Anthony chafed over D'Antoni's trust of Lin with the ball and clashed with the coach. In the inevitable showdown, Dolan sided with *his* premier acquisition at the expense of an out-of-nowhere marketing sensation. Long-suffering and implausibly loyal Knicks fans were stiffed again, a year after ponying up price increases that had averaged 49 percent. In July 2012, Dolan ordered his front office not to match an offer Lin had received from the Houston Rockets after some eleventh-hour bookkeeping elevated the stakes and guaranteed Lin a bigger score. Dolan, who had shelled out staggering sums for underwhelming players with no box office appeal, was furious. He had his minions portray Lin as an ingrate. One steaming-mad longtime ticket holder I quoted in my column didn't see it that way:

> After sitting there all those years and watching all that horrible basketball, we finally had such a feel-good story that felt like our own. How many times can they hurt me?

For the first time, Michelle refused to put her name on a quote. Whereas she had been a public voice of the beleaguered fan, eager to be heard in newspaper columns, she was now understandably fearful of losing her choice location, fully aware of how vindictive Dolan and his people could be with employees and fans, not just reporters. Bad basketball was hard enough to stomach, but Michelle was now having to go underground in complaining about it.

"So why do you continue going?" I asked her.

"Oh, I don't know," she said. "I always think, maybe there'll be a miracle."

Through the Anthony years, she hoped in vain. With the exception of a fifty-four-win season that produced one playoff series victory in the 2013 postseason, they were ordinary at best, unwatchable at worst, especially after Phil Jackson arrived in 2014 as general manager. The Hall of Fame coach was a rookie executive, pushing seventy, coaxed out of retirement by a $60 million haul and another pledge of noninterference from Dolan. Jackson soon handed Anthony a rich new contract that included a bewildering no-trade clause.

Michelle was beside herself. "Why?" she kept asking me. Even with a pipeline to Jackson based on knowing him since the late seventies, I had no rational explanation, other than it being his gesture of gratitude to Dolan for his own lucrative contract (which ultimately became a de facto golden parachute from the sport when Jackson was canned in 2017). Somewhat fittingly, the immediate result of Anthony's new deal was the worst Knicks season in history, a descent so deep into the league's basement that even the drafting of the promising Kristaps Porzingis couldn't pull the team out.

Dolan's subversion of Walsh and acquisition of Anthony set the team back a decade, and Jackson's decision to slog on with him as a resident star only delayed and complicated the inevitable overhaul, blurring more seasons of competitive despair and wasting time that Michelle didn't have.

Wynn Plaut couldn't be expected to subsidize her forever. She never indulged herself with notions of a triumphant departure, the way the great athletes did. It was still sobering to have to acknowledge that her four-plus decades at the Garden would conclude not only championship-less, but competitively hapless.

From time to time, I would insist to Michelle that Anthony—though more concerned with personal branding than with winning a title—was actually a pretty good guy, who had, like Stoudemire, welcomed the challenge of New York. There was no convincing her of that, though. Operating from inside his superstar cocoon, Anthony was not one to commune with her or any fan. He was probably her least favorite player in all her time at courtside, but I argued with her that he was who he was, and he hadn't acquired himself. In the final analysis, there should have been only one man to blame. Ultimately, Michelle knew this, too. "The day Dolan made Donnie get Carmelo," she said, "was for me the death of all hope."

In February 2017, Michelle was in her final season as the holder of her Knicks tickets, and Porzingis's development was one of the only reasons to be excited about where the team was headed. Early in a game against the Los Angeles Clippers, Porzingis was at the free-throw line. As he prepared to shoot, it became clear that some kind of commotion was breaking out in the stands just behind the basket he faced, a couple of rows behind James Dolan.

I was sitting high atop the court in the press area on the Garden's eighth level. From the media's vantage point, it was not easy to determine what the fuss was about—security guards rushing over, converging on a tall man in a dark suit with salt-and-pepper hair, who seemed to be in the middle of the fracas. Fans in the area were standing, craning their necks to see what was happening.

Someone down the row from me, apparently with much clearer vision, yelled out, "Holy shit, is that Oakley?" And soon came a confirming chant from below of the old warrior's name—"Oakley, Oakley"—as the unfathomable unfolded below. The Knicks' beloved enforcer of the nineties, Patrick Ewing's unofficial bodyguard, was wrestled to the ground, cuffed, and dragged out, the crowd continuing its chant as if Oakley's adversaries were Scottie Pippen and Horace Grant.

A statement was soon released by the Knicks, alleging that "Charles Oakley came to the game tonight and behaved in a highly inappropriate and completely abusive manner. He has been ejected and is currently being arrested by the New York City Police Department. He was a great Knick and we hope he gets some help soon."

It was no secret that Oakley had for years had a prickly relationship with Dolan, whose arrival on the scene in 1999 had coincided with his being traded to Toronto. Oakley, cranky by nature, was thus a rare former Knick who had no problem publicly calling Dolan and the franchise out for their chronic dysfunction. He had been just as outspoken as a player, once criticizing Ewing, his teammate, for allowing the 1998 lockout to drag on as the players' union president. Oakley's complaints were never mean-spirited, or even calculated; they were just stream-of-consciousness kvetching. But in retirement, his style violated Dolan's loyalty code.

Michelle loved Oakley for all he had physically sacrificed to the Garden's cause. She always would tell me that while Ewing was the team's unquestioned star, Oakley, in all his orneriness, was its backbone. And unlike Ewing, Oakley shared his thoughts with the fans—including her—much as he did with the writers. Their rapport carried over to his post-playing years. Before the feud with Dolan turned nasty, he often sat in Michelle's section when attending a game. He would stop by to chat about the team, Michelle understanding half of what Oakley, who typically spoke in bursts of accelerated garbles, was saying. When he occasionally suggested they have lunch, she knew it would never happen. She was still flattered by the thought.

I knew Michelle had to have been horrified by the humiliation Oakley had endured in the arena he loved most. And I sure as hell wasn't going to take the Knicks' word for why it had occurred. At halftime, I raced down to courtside and asked her how much, if any, of the scuffle she had seen. One more time, my courtside source clued me in.

Nothing unusual had happened until the security people appeared and tried to make Oakley leave, she said. The Knicks contended that Oakley was belligerent and profane from the moment he entered the arena, yelling at Dolan from a seat he had apparently purchased from a season-ticket owner. But when footage of the episode surfaced, it appeared to corroborate Michelle's contention that Oakley, while laughing and joking with fans, hadn't created a scene at all until Dolan, caught on video, summoned security to have him removed.

There was, of course, no defending Oakley's shoving a much smaller security guard, touching off the melee. It was also possible that, literally behind Dolan's back, he had said *something* offensive that was loud enough to hear. But the issue, once again, was how little it obviously took to set off Dolan. The video evidence was clear that the episode might have been avoided had Dolan been more circumspect. He just couldn't resist the temptation to make an uncomfortable situation much, much worse. His crassness came through loud and clear when he went on the radio and offered a familiar depiction of an adversary, alleging that Oakley was a drunk.

When I called Michelle a couple of days later, she was again incredulous at Dolan's complete tone deafness to the chaos that he—more than anyone—was responsible for. She dismissed the Knicks' side of the story. "I know what I saw," she said. The dysfunction had been unfolding in front of her for far too long. Even in her subsidized seat, the price of watching it was becoming too steep.

Ten
·············

The Long View

After the trepidation of accepting the position as a columnist in the Sports of the Times rotation gave way to excitement, actually writing the column was akin to minding a hyperactive toddler: an endless chase. Every day brought a manic monitoring of the sports landscape for a kernel of an idea. And even when breaking news provided the material on a platter, I was still seized with guilt about leaving too many domestic issues to Beth, who had her own professional obligations. Nights at home and weekend plans with the kids ended abruptly with a call from the office, demanding a quick take on the Yankees' latest free-agent acquisition or the steroid bust of the week. My sons grew up with Daddy drifting off in deep next-column contemplation at dinner. Or entirely begging off a meal to head to the ballpark. Or maniacally rushing home from the airport after a dawn flight from Somewhere, USA, to catch the second half of a youth soccer game, only to arrive after the final whistle.

There were payoffs for the boys, for sure—trips to spring training, NBA All-Star weekends, and a natural connection to the iconic subjects of schoolboy conversation, from Michael Jordan to Derek Jeter to Eli Manning. On long Olympic trips to Europe and beyond in the years just before video conferencing, there were AOL chat-room connections with their classrooms from their sportswriter dad. But the work demands were inevitably expressed in a variety of less-flattering personality tics. Before I knew it, I *became* my column, test-driving ideas with anyone willing to listen, dropping lines like a comedian prowling for a laugh backstage before facing a tough crowd. "Good one, Dad," Alex, my elder son, would smirk when I rehearsed on family time. "Now I don't have to read the paper tomorrow."

It only got worse in the age of social media and the encouraged interaction with readers that was often unpleasant but also, I discovered, somewhat addictive. And as much as I bitched about those who *didn't get it*, worse was awakening the morning after a column was posted online with no reactions to it at all. Inevitably, the column became a reliable measure of not only achievement but also relevance. Churning out three and sometimes four a week could be exhausting, but at the same time, I only once came close to bailing on the column, briefly mulling a move to the Metro desk after the 2002 Winter Olympics. Three weeks in a Salt Lake City Holiday Inn was enough to make anyone at least briefly consider career recalibration. Ultimately, as with most of my colleagues at the *Times* and elsewhere, I viewed the column as a lifetime appointment, like a seat on the Supreme Court—at least until the spring of 2009, when my editors summoned me to inform me otherwise.

I had sensed in the previous months that *something* was brewing at the *Times* in relation to the sports column. Dave Anderson had retired. Selena Roberts had left to join *Sports Illustrated*. Neither had been replaced. At the 2008 Summer Olympics in Beijing, the Sports of the Times column—written by me or by George Vecsey—seemed to be routinely buried on the website. And I had seen accomplished columnists at other papers relieved of their status, and in some cases their jobs. Still, how could I not take it personally when Tom Jolly, the sports editor, sat me down and said that I didn't seem enthusiastic about the column in the way I had been in previous years, and perhaps it was time for a change. It was also soon clear that this was no suggestion. I was stunned, bewildered, crushed. It felt like a thief had broken into my house in the middle of the night and made off with not only my laptop, but my identity. Hadn't I devoted myself enough? Sacrificed enough time on the road? Taken on the most challenging deadlines, year after year? My instinct was survivalist—I pushed back at the assertion that I was no longer "enthusiastic" enough.

As if my wounded pride was not enough, worse was the sudden specter of dramatic change—writing for the paper's features sections—in a spiraling economy and in a newspaper industry herding writers and editors like so many sheep to slaughter. I was fifty-six, with one son finishing his freshman year of college and another in high school. I convinced myself that I was being set up to fail.

Michelle didn't disagree with my belief that top editors at the *Times* beyond Jolly—none of them the same people who had hired and promoted me—had likely come to view my work, or at least my role at the newspaper, differently. In her experience in dealing with corporate hierarchies, she recognized that no removal of an employee with a high-profile position like the one I'd had for fifteen years would fail to have the stamp of approval from the very top—in this case, the masthead. Having been left with five kids and no sustainable means of support, she was the last person to minimize my fears of being able to pay the bills. But as an expert on corporate strategy when it came to personnel maneuverings, she wasn't quite ready to indulge me on the prospect of imminent dismissal and financial ruin. More likely, she said, the *Times* was testing me—how flexible could I be? Was I a team player? Would I continue working hard even after the loss of the column?

We sipped wine in her living room, where she reminded me of other work crises and self-imposed panics I'd survived. In 2001, I had written a book about Beth and her friends having taken up soccer for the first time as adults. What had begun as an upbeat women's-empowerment project about a spirited band of Montclair moms discovering the joys and challenges of team sports had taken a dramatic narrative turn when the group's organizer left her husband for a young English soccer trainer. By then, I had developed a pretty thick skin when the well-paid professionals I covered objected to a column I had written. But these women were not used to such detailed public scrutiny. They were also neighbors and friends—mainly of Beth's. As the date of publication neared, I worried about how they would respond and, if negatively, would they hold it against her? Had my career ambitions been served to the detriment of my wife's personal life? In advance of a visit around publication time—as it turned out, a few days before 9/11—Michelle suggested that I bring along a copy and asked me to read her the parts that I considered most salacious. After every few sentences, she would interrupt and ask, "What is so terrible about that?"

Read aloud, it did all sound reasonably and sensitively presented. Maybe I wasn't such an exploitative asshole after all. "You told the story, you wrote what happened, and it sounds to me like you bent over backwards to be as uncontroversial about it as possible." Of course, Michelle knew something about an insular community turning on one of its own. She survived and so did I. In the end, the book was generally well received around town. I moved on, chiding myself for overreacting and promising myself to keep things in perspective—to not make a habit of inflating matters that were not life-and-death.

But the work crisis had spooked me in a different, deeper way. Among the new sections I would be expected to write for were Sunday Real Estate, the now-defunct Home and Garden, and Sunday Styles. Styles? How *stylish* was I—a graying suburban dad? The more I thought about it, the more I convinced myself I was a doomed man, with only months left to work.

"So what do you want to do?" Michelle said.

"I don't know, maybe just refuse to change departments and risk being laid off at the end of the year."

"If you do that, you won't be *risking* a layoff—it'll be guaranteed," she said. "And who will you end up punishing, the *Times* or yourself?"

I nodded, the answer obvious.

"And if you show up and give it your best shot, what's the downside of that?" she said.

I sighed and laughed—at myself, for being too predictable a patient for Dr. Musler to psychoanalyze.

"That I'll suck at it."

"So after all that you've done, you're back to being afraid to fail," she said. "Wasn't that why you hesitated about doing the column in the first place? Now you're furious that they want you to try something else again—but how did getting out of your comfort zone work out for you last time?"

"It worked out."

"It didn't just work out—it worked out great," she said. "So why not give this a chance to work out, too?"

She wasn't too modest to remind me that back in the day she had professionally reinvented herself under far greater pressure. She'd had no obvious career path—and also no choice. While my circumstances weren't quite so dire, I didn't either, as Michelle reminded me via email:

WELL, YOU MIGHT BE ABLE TO DO THIS BY REMEMBERING WHAT CAUSES THE ANXIETY—FEAR OF CHANGE, FEAR OF FAILURE. RECOGNIZING THE TRIGGER SYMPTOMS AND LEARNING HOW TO CONTROL THEM MIGHT HELP YOU RESTORE SOME BALANCE.

I pushed forward, managed to not only accept the new role but put on my best professional face. Within a few weeks, my churning emotions gave way to old ambitions. I found my footing—and a new lease on journalism life. My first story for the feature team, reported for Home and Garden, was about the burden placed on families forced to downsize during a painful recession—an idea hatched by my own fears of pending financial upheaval. (For once, those fears were good for something!)

I found a family in central Connecticut that had been forced to downsize to a modest, cramped home from the opulent house of their dreams. Much like the women in my soccer moms book—and unlike the athletes I was accustomed to covering—the family presented with honesty and without shame their inner turmoil over perceived failure and hardship. The story was not only well received, it provoked a heated online debate in the comments section over the guilt expressed by the parents and the indignation of the children, along with an invitation from the *Times* to do a podcast. A ribbing email from Michelle dropped on the day the story appeared:

SO WHAT ARE YOU GOING TO SAY YOU CAN'T DO NEXT?

Next, I wrote a piece about how visitors to New York from abroad were obsessed with the HBO megahit *The Sopranos*, and how, of all places, the bowels of New Jersey, where many scenes from the show had been shot, had become a popular tourist attraction. I delivered a personalized front-page account to Sunday Real Estate about my dumping of a troubled Brooklyn Heights co-op that not long after was worth much, much more—a cathartic piece that helped me get over seller's remorse and not want to set fire to the *Times*'s real estate section whenever it listed a similar neighborhood apartment for five times the amount I had sold mine for. But my eureka moment occurred when I pitched a story on why fifty-something-year-olds would subject themselves to drills from masochistic young trainers by enrolling in adult tennis camps. I was given a budget that allowed me to take a partner—Beth—to a Florida resort for a few days to interview attendees and smack a few balls under the warm winter sun. Aches and all, I had an epiphany as I lounged by the pool between sessions with a cool drink in my hand: This wasn't such a bad gig after all.

The upshot was that I was rediscovering the pleasures of in-depth storytelling—as opposed to hasty formulations of sports-related short takes. I was also working more normal hours instead of scrambling from one airport to another and enduring the nocturnal trials of late-night events—a change that was refreshing, not to mention fairer to and easier on family.

But about a year after leaving Sports, I was told that the feature-writing team was being disbanded to strengthen sections hit by staff reductions that did not, thankfully, include me. I negotiated a return to Sports in a hybrid position. I no longer had the Sports of the Times title, but I could still write columns when I had something to say while pursuing long-form enterprise reporting. It didn't take long for me to realize that I now had the best of both creative worlds, and who cared what my job title was? Most readers never noticed the difference.

The truth was that the sports-media landscape had changed entirely in just a few short years. The smart, nuanced, well-reported column was still for me as a reader the best anchor to a sports section or site—and there remained plenty of damn good ones around the country. But as online metrics raised the profile of the news-breaking, sport-specific insider, the generalist had become a hunted species by editors wielding the ax under never-ending pressure to reduce staff. In the age of social media and the continuous reel of cable network yak-fests, quick takes were the rage. To survive, much less thrive, the conventional newspaper columnist needed to be part journalist, part self-promoter—a brand with a mass following on Twitter and, ideally, multiple platforms. There had been a time during the nineties when opportunities to transition into television presented themselves, but that wasn't for me. I was on the road too much as it was. When I was home, I preferred to spend nights reading to my young boys, not sitting in a green room waiting to regurgitate what I'd already written in a column.

Now, I had lost the Sports of the Times column, but I had also come unstuck from a state of complacency—and in turn was inspired to the most productive years of my career. With renewed energy, I began teaching journalism classes as an adjunct at Montclair State University. I wrote a book on the championship Knicks teams of the seventies—with Michelle's name appearing on the dedication page—that became an ESPN *30 for 30* documentary film. An A-1 *Times* feature story I wrote on the loving intergenerational relationship between the Yankees greats Yogi Berra and Ron Guidry led to a book that became a *Times* bestseller. A novel I had finished a rough first draft of—a father-son story based on the *Daily News* strike—was published by a small press after a rigorous reimagining and rewriting. In a fairly accurate measure of her loyalty as well as my proficiency at fiction, Michelle bought enough copies to account for roughly half the sales.

Still, a published novel, regardless of how successful, was a bucket list item for me, one I was hugely proud of. "So what are you going to complain about now?" Michelle cracked while she had me sign copies for her family and friends. I laughed and admitted, if only for the moment, "I got nothing."

In any honest retrospective, the loss of the column was certainly no reward and no trivial matter in the context of what it had represented to have written it in the first place. But what had occurred in the aftermath and the eventual reversal of fortune was my reward for rejecting both martyrdom and fear. For playing the hand I was dealt, as best I could—and for heeding the advice of the woman who had survived her share of strife, pretty much on her own, with the help of a psychiatrist but without the benefit of a special friend like herself.

What Michelle had learned, and what she routinely reminded me, was: "Complaining is a waste of time—and it gets you nowhere."

Though she continued to claim that her cognitive skills were eroding and her memory failing, Michelle was still reading, still contemplating, still making connections. On the morning of February 27, 2018, she emailed me.

HI HARVEY . . . BE SURE TO READ, IF YOU ALREADY HAVEN'T, THE SUNDAY REVIEW SECTION—FIRST PAGE. 'AM I GOING BLIND,' BY FRANK BRUNI.

I had, in fact, already read Bruni's column in the *Times*, in which he disclosed that he suffered from a rare condition that in all likelihood had permanently compromised the vision in his right eye, leaving him feeling, as he wrote, "drunk without being drunk, dizzy but not exactly dizzy." The headline had leapt off my computer screen and filled me with a familiar dread. Bruni, one of the newspaper's Op-Ed regulars, was fifty-three when he was diagnosed with nonarteritic anterior ischemic optic neuropathy, which affects one in ten thousand Americans. Without warning, a man whose life was invested in printed and digitized words was calculating the chances—roughly 20 percent—that the condition could eventually afflict his left eye as well. In other words, that he could go blind. As it turned out, I now lived with the same fear.

My condition was the far more common macular degeneration, which attacks the central vision of people typically over fifty in stages—early, intermediate, and advanced. In early 2016, months shy of my sixty-fourth birthday, my optometrist had delivered the frightening news about a sudden slight blurring in my right eye.

"You won't get that back," she told me. Over time, she added, because macular degeneration is a progressive disease typically found in both eyes, my vision would likely be further compromised.

"How long?" I asked.

"Impossible to know," she said.

She promised only that my life would not soon change, but that reassuring prognosis did not last long. Three months later, I was covering the 2016 NBA Finals in Oakland when straight lines on my computer screen began to flutter. Newspaper print appeared to be dancing. At a pre-series press conference, NBA commissioner Adam Silver's face vanished into a featureless gray canvas when someone blocked my left line of vision to the front of the room.

Terrified, I flew home and learned that my condition had converted from dry macular degeneration—a general atrophying that normally takes years to worsen—to what is known as the wet version. Leaky blood vessels left unattended would cause scarring and accelerated blindness if I wasn't immediately treated. This meant injections into my eye several times a year for the rest of my life. As if that wasn't awful enough, the vision in my right eye had already deteriorated to no better than 20/80. I was told that the medication would stabilize it with a roughly 30 percent possibility of some restoration.

The injections, more pinch than pain, were the least of it. Far more unnerving was the "emotional riddle," as Bruni described it. How do you rest easy while knowing that you will awaken to uncertainty—the possibility of a world permanently blurred or darkened? He tried to cope by ritualizing his doctor's suggestion that he stay hydrated, especially before bedtime. Dark humor with family and friends provided moments of relief from persistent flashes of fright. Prayer—the best advice his doctor could offer—did little to comfort a nonreligious man.

"I'm better at drama," Bruni admitted. I could relate, and anyone who knew me well would be moved to say amen.

I did try to laugh it off as best I could, linking my eye condition to a relatively minor prostate procedure I had also undergone to claim that my life had essentially come down to "seeing and peeing." But good luck putting a consistently happy face on potential blindness. My habit of catastrophizing sudden adversity ultimately won out, and it had occurred enough times by this stage of my adult life to call it by its clinical name: episodic depression and anxiety, typically symptomized by sleep deprivation and a loss of appetite and confidence. In retrospect, I could cop to the plea that I had overreacted to most of my prior life crises, and all of these chapters were, in essence, merely detours along a successful and relatively steady-as-she-goes journey. But at the time, they felt like cause for real despair.

It's a terrible place to be, awakening each morning with a crippling lethargy and unshakable foreboding. Work suffers. Relationships fray. Simple tasks can feel like a massive undertaking. Fortunately, these periods tended not to last long, blessed as I was with a loving wife and sons, good friends, and the ability to lift myself up with therapy, exercise, and ultimately my work. And, of course, there was always Michelle, my fortifying go-to voice of experience and reason—caring but never too accommodating.

A therapist's goal is to create a road map to self-discovery, the more conventional and presumably more lasting means of psychological growth. But Michelle was no shrink, even if she wholeheartedly endorsed psychotherapy, valuing the work of her psychiatrist, Dr. Goldfarb, during her solo-parenting years to the point where she visited him out west years after he'd retired from his practice. But in Michelle's line of work, *dealing with* a person's problems was a more urgent end than *healing*. She didn't have time to nurture clients through some tortured process of self-discovery. Her job was to lay out the truth, whether or not the person in question wanted to hear it.

Her friends were treated no differently, even if they weren't obligated to listen. Whine for a few moments if you must, she would say, but I sure as hell am not going to encourage you to wallow. When Robin Kelly's marriage to Wynn Plaut was ending, her therapist went so far as to suggest that she steer clear of Michelle, who had been characteristically brusque when assessing the terms of the divorce. To wit: Stop bitching about it. Given Michelle's own marriage-ending experience, Robin had made out like a bandit: an amicable parting, generous financial settlement, a prize Manhattan apartment. Why ruminate? Why waste time when you could be getting on with life? Robin eventually asked that her therapist back off—she actually didn't want to feel sorry for herself. She could handle the truth and appreciated Michelle's giving it to her, however bluntly.

I was no different. During the early, dispiriting weeks after my macular degeneration diagnosis and through the shock of the conversion to the condition's more troubling wet form, it was Michelle's tough medicine that somehow provided me the most comfort. It calmed—or actually steeled—me more than any medical reassurance, sympathy from family and friends, or even commiseration from my mother, bless her, whose advanced macular degeneration from her mid-eighties into her early nineties had left her unable to read or make out faces from more than a few feet away.

I suppose it was a testament to the trust I had in Michelle, her credibility and consistency. While others would assure me, "Oh, you'll be fine," she would only tell me that maybe I would and maybe I wouldn't—I'd just have to push it all aside and figure out a way to deal with my fate when the time came. Because, again, what choice did I have?

It was an example of what I most admired about Michelle—how she pressed forward, even as daunting life changes occurred. As powerful as her backstory was, as much as she had persevered, her resolve in later years made an even more powerful impression on me because I got to witness it firsthand. As she aged, Michelle was determined to do whatever was necessary to maintain her career—including defying Father Time with the assistance of a cosmetic surgeon. The night I turned around from my press row seat at the Garden and found her looking several years younger seems in retrospect like a potential scene from *Curb Your Enthusiasm*. Was it my imagination? The lighting in the arena? A miracle of makeup? Even for the congenitally indiscreet Larry David, this would have been a tricky ask.

"You look great, Michelle," I stammered, choosing tact over temerity and hoping she would let me in on her secret.

"Thank you," she said. "I paid enough for it."

In a more private setting, she told me she had undergone the nip-and-tuck as a calculated career investment. Some of her clients were aging out or dying, and were being replaced by younger executives. As much as she resented the double standards for women, especially older women, they were what they were. She had convinced herself that she needed to appear more youthful to extend her career. She liked looking good, too.

Her strategy worked out for a while, but her own health issues intervened, requiring prolonged absences for one surgery or another. Michelle's 2001 Christmas letter in the year of her sixty-fifth birthday brought evidence of her first work crisis since she had launched her corporate career three decades earlier at Xerox:

> *Executive coaching and development has been*
> *outstanding (even with commuting to California*
> *regularly) until this July when it slowed and remains*

slow. Traditionally, the summer has not been a slow
period for me. Difficult to know if I should relax and
enjoy the much-needed downtime or stay awake every
night contemplating which bridge I should jump off.
Throgs Neck and Tappan Zee are the leading contenders.
They are the most scenic.

Not long after—exhausted by a weather-plagued journey that resulted in "three days in the air going nowhere," for a client who didn't show up once Michelle had reached her destination, "Idaho freaking Falls"—she made the decision to eliminate travel from her schedule. She was tired of the chase and sick of pushing back on the jerks who reclined in front of her in coach class. But in downsizing her business, she more or less sealed its fate. Traveling was as essential to Michelle's work as it was to mine. Clients began to drift away; relationships dried up. Without ever formally announcing her retirement, she began transitioning into the next phase of her life. She handled it not without any wistfulness, or worry, but mostly with the same pragmatism that she had handled every other situation she'd been faced with. With the time and freedom to do what she pleased, she gradually replaced professional hours with personal interests. Before too long, she was thinking, *Isn't this wonderful?*

Almost fifteen years after her last company report was filed, she still claimed never to have been bored a day in her life. And even without ownership of Knicks tickets, there still were games, always the games—the Knicks or whatever else the NBA served up on its partner networks—to get her through dark winter nights.

Like anyone else, she experienced bouts of frustration, of sorrow. I remained convinced that her brief depression during the 2017–18 holidays was the residual effect of no longer going regularly to the Garden. But she clearly had moved on from that emotional rut and was back to embracing the belief that having a clean daily slate was the upside of aging, the comforting freedom to take life one day at a time, while trying not to dwell on what was too far ahead.

Who at a certain age, she asked when I expressed fears about not being able to read or write in the future, is guaranteed anything more than what they are doing in the moment? Which got me to thinking: Who more than the young athletes I had been covering for decades was at the mercy of limited time, of their bodies being one ligament tear from career limbo, or worse?

Just weeks before Bruni's column appeared, Michelle's newest favorite Knick, Kristaps Porzingis, had landed with a thud and fallen awkwardly to the Garden floor, curled up in the fetal position. Had she been in her courtside seat that night, she would have had a perfect view of the crash—Porzingis cutting down the lane, taking a bounce pass, dunking in the basket nearest the Knicks' bench over Milwaukee's Giannis Antetokounmpo, another of the league's rising young international stars. But she was on her living room sofa, watching the heartbreaking replays of Porzingis's left knee tearing to shreds. Even at home, there was no escaping the Knicks' rotten luck and no missing the sad irony—along with the one tiny measure of wicked satisfaction—of the injury occurring practically at the feet of James Dolan.

I was in South Florida visiting a friend and was alerted to Porzingis's injury on Twitter soon after it happened. On cue, an email arrived the next morning from Michelle: "BERNARD KING ALL OVER AGAIN." Yes, and no. Advances in surgical technique had greatly improved the odds of complete recovery after what typically was a year of recovery and rehab for a torn ACL. But questions loomed—would Porzingis return with the same uncommon athleticism for a man seven foot three? Would he run and jump with carefree abandon? Who knew? But Bruni's column, lovingly shared by Michelle, offered needed perspective. A filmmaker whose documentary had chronicled his vision loss from glaucoma told Bruni, "You cannot spend your life preparing for future losses." Bruni himself concluded, "It disrespects the blessings of the here and now."

Michelle's email about the Bruni column was part of her ongoing campaign to impress upon me the state of uncertainty in which we all lived. Bruni, a decade younger, clearly agonized over the possibility of losing his career. For me, at a later stage, uncertainty about my physical condition influenced my thoughts about when the right time would be to discontinue my full-time journalist's life.

I had relished my many years of covering sports—the unmatched drama, the possibility every night of witnessing something special. As a *Times* columnist, I had especially grown to appreciate the power of sports to address social and cultural issues, far more than using my forum for screeds to fire the coach.

The upscale readership I had once feared would reject me as not smart or informed enough had—for the most part—accepted me as part of its daily consumption of sports commentary. Yet working in a world of mind-numbingly rich young people who were less and less receptive to the idea of reporters nosing around required a growing, gnawing suspension of reality. They and their handlers, more and more mainly interested in speaking in clichés for the television cameras, dictated the terms. I was tiring of those terms and of airports—security lines, delays, cancellations, leg room for Lilliputians. When the *Times* offered buyouts from late spring into the summer of 2016, only months after my eye diagnosis and weeks after my first injection, the deal was too tempting to pass up.

Would I have reached the same conclusion had I not just been through the emotional ringer? If I'd had a clearer window into the foreseeable future? Impossible to say, even in retrospect. But as hard as career decisions had always been for me, this was one I managed to reach with a dispassionate, almost rudimentary ease. This surprised those who knew me best—especially Michelle, who kept promising that there would be plenty for me to do, not to worry. The truth was, I *wasn't* worried, and I found myself in a rare Zen-like state, immensely gratified with the last stretch of years at the *Times*. I could admit—to myself and even to Tom Jolly, the editor who had presided over my removal from the Sports of the Times lineup—that I probably had needed a change, a reboot. My editors had recognized something in me that I hadn't. They had, for whatever reason, done me a favor.

At my farewell toast, a *Times* newsroom tradition, I found myself wanting to tell my younger colleagues to appreciate the ride more, that in the final analysis, I had come to the realization that I had few, if any, regrets and no serious complaints. Was I kidding? Telling a pro forma lie in light of an occasion that included Beth and my boys by my side? I don't think so.

If a state of contentment was a rarity for the typical sports journalist, it was practically unheard of for me. There were more than a few folks in my audience who had indulged my grumblings about editors, assignments, and other grievances through the years. One of them, Selena Roberts, had hilariously dubbed me Sir Whines-a-Lot during one rainy afternoon in the Wimbledon media workroom. Filip Bondy, my old friend and colleague from the *Daily News* and briefly the *Times*, as well as a Montclair neighbor, told me afterward that he was dying to get up and tell all those toasting me, "At one time or another, Harvey has complained about every one of you."

Who was this new cheerful, self-fulfilled guy? I wasn't quite sure myself, but I hoped he might stick around. And I knew that in no small part I owed his existence to Michelle.

Eleven

The End Game

As the winter of 2018 gave way to spring, I phoned Michelle to say that Beth and I would be having Sunday brunch in Greenwich with an old family friend. Would she be around later for a drop-by?

"Just you or Beth, too?" she said.

"Both."

Michelle sounded thrilled. Seldom leaving Stamford, unwilling to drive much beyond her neighborhood, she saw fewer people these days. It also had been a while since she had seen my better half—about eighteen months, at the funeral of Beth's father, just thirteen months after we had buried her mother. It had been years since Beth had spent much quality time with Michelle, going back to her Christmas Eve parties or the occasional holiday dinner at my in-laws' home in Greenwich. Still, I always sensed their mutual affection. Michelle loved hearing about Beth's midlife transition from sports public relations to education and her role as a union activist, fighting for teachers and against corporate annexation of public schools. Not surprisingly, she admired tenacious women with a cause but, more selfishly, she appreciated how Beth was never threatened by how much I confided in her or resentful of the time I devoted to the friendship. Even the hour or two I invariably stole from in-law visits was never an issue. Michelle especially was flattered when I told her how Beth had made it clear to her parents that she, for me, was family, too.

We arrived at her condo in the midafternoon and sat on her L-shaped living room couch, sipping wine, catching up, Michelle apologizing in advance for any memory lapses she might have, as she now tended to. Just that week, she said, she had confused the days, mistaken Thursday for Saturday, and missed three appointments: a lunch date, a yoga class, and therapy for her latest malady, a sore rotator cuff. Her accountant had also called to tell her she had made a mess of her tax filings and he would have to come by to help put them in order. "He obviously doesn't trust me anymore to get the numbers right," she said. "But the neurologist told me I should expect that as I move a little closer to dementia." She sighed. "It is what it is."

Michelle had made few concessions in her daily routine beyond the sporadic use of a cane and a senior alert necklace. She was still stubbornly navigating the stairs in her condo, albeit slowly. Her attendance at yoga classes—in all likelihood the cause of her rotator cuff pain—was steady. She concentrated harder when reading and watching television but remained committed to the byzantine plotlines of her favorite Showtime programs, *Billions* and *Homeland*. Much as she knew she would be worse off for it, she couldn't resist tuning in to cable news at night to recoil over the state of American politics and fret over the future of the republic—for which on occasion she expressed sardonic relief that she probably wouldn't have to endure too much of. Thank goodness, she said, there was Trevor Noah, her new TV hero, to put a comic spin on it all.

Despite a determined but futile tutorial from me during almost every visit, she was hopelessly befuddled by the smartphone she had talked herself into buying, but was still backing her Subaru out of her narrow driveway and into the cramped space between the condos across the way. She tired earlier and was following her doctor's advice to not answer the phone at night, but that apparently wasn't keeping her from staying up late to watch Noah or a good NBA game.

She lately was fixated on a Boston-Houston cliffhanger she had stuck with despite it ending close to midnight. The game was already weeks old, but watching Mike D'Antoni coach the high-scoring Rockets—in the process of compiling the best record in the league—had only aggravated her feelings about his Carmelo Anthony–orchestrated departure from the Knicks. "Still drives me crazy that Mike left and Carmelo stayed," she said.

This prompted an impassioned diatribe about Anthony and James Dolan, with Beth listening in amazement and me nodding in agreement. "You keep saying you can't remember things, but everything you remember I've already forgotten," I said. That made her laugh.

One thing was clear to me: With Michelle, there was no comparison to the heartbreaking deterioration Beth and I had experienced with her parents—her mother's Alzheimer's and her father's dementia. As Beth's father had done in the grip of the disease, Michelle occasionally would point an index finger to the side of her head when a certain word eluded her. Unlike my father-in-law, whose short-term memory grew so lacking that he would forget a conversation minutes after it occurred, Michelle's recall, both distant and recent, was still quite good. Her questions to Beth about her work were specific. She remembered the career paths of our sons, Alex and Charly. By name she identified Beth's mother's dearest friend, the woman we had brunched with in Greenwich, despite my having mentioned the name, Sylvia, only in passing when I had called about visiting the previous day.

She also expressed vivid memories of our wedding reception on the front lawn of my in-laws' home and of a call she had made to Beth's father during the early eighties to tell him that the young attorney he had just hired happened to be her new daughter-in-law. It was the first of several coincidental intersections of our family's arcs. The last and most delightful was Charly and one of Michelle's two grandsons winding up one grade apart at Clark University in Worcester, Massachusetts, a small school made smaller by basketball; Andrew was a varsity player, Charly on the club team. They occasionally ran together in full-court pickup games. It had thrilled Michelle that both her grandsons had played high school ball and that Andrew had gone on to star on the Clark team. We had made a plan at one point to take a drive together to watch one of his games, but the boys' college years went by in a flash, while Michelle grew less mobile. We never did make the trip.

Before another horrendous Knicks season could mercifully draw to a close, Michelle made one more trek to the Garden. She attended an early April 2018 game with Wynn Plaut—her fourth of the season, one of thousands across forty-five seasons.

There was little worth remembering about it, other than that the Knicks lost once again. With Kristaps Porzingis injured, they would drop twenty-five of their last thirty-one games of the 2017–18 season. Looming was another unceremonious firing of a coach (Jeff Hornacek). The tally of consecutive years missing the playoffs would grow to five for the NBA team with the worst cumulative record of the twenty-first century. Michelle couldn't help herself, though. She had never been a fair-weather fan, Plaut had been gracious enough to not only offer but to drive her into city—and who knew when, or if, another opportunity would arise?

"I don't know what's going to happen next season," she told the security guard who for years had presided over her section, while giving him a hug. If she never made it back, this would be her proper good-bye. The next day, she told me that schlepping into the city to watch this pitiful team no longer served her in the way it had in the past. Much as she loved her courtside view, the conclusion of recent Knicks seasons had actually become a relief from the blur of meaningless games and being surrounded in her section mostly by strangers.

Absent the Knicks, the playoffs had become Michelle's time to appreciate the game at its best in her twilight years. She looked forward to two compelling months of authentic NBA drama, night in, night out—without having to get off the couch to enjoy it.

I had suggested Sunday, April 15, for a visit because the Oklahoma City Thunder was scheduled to play Game 1 of a first-round playoff series against the Utah Jazz. Michelle was less a fan of the Thunder than she had been when Kevin Durant was costarring with Russell Westbrook; and when Scott Brooks, her buddy from his brief days of riding the Knicks bench, was coach. She still loved watching Westbrook for his sheer athleticism and unbridled aggression, despite my reminding her that her choice of a favorite NBA player was a bit of a contradiction. Westbrook, during crucial points of a game, could be as much of a spirit-killing ball hog as Carmelo Anthony. She ignored my comparative assessment. Michelle liked what she liked. And I had to admit that Westbrook played with a hunger that Anthony never had.

But as if the Knicks hadn't tormented her enough, when they finally did trade Anthony, they had sent him to the Thunder to partner with Westbrook and Paul George. Michelle immediately predicted that he would ruin the Thunder the way he ruined the Knicks. Lo and behold, Anthony was the same defensive liability for the Thunder, proved uncomfortable and unproductive without the ball in an offense controlled by Westbrook, and pushed back indignantly against the sensible notion of a reduced, non-starter's role.

Back at Michelle's, we watched the Thunder take Game 1 behind Westbrook and George, but they would go on to lose the series, with Anthony proving every point Michelle had ever made about him in the fourth quarter of Game 5. Oblivious to the Thunder's tighter defense without him on the floor, he argued on the sideline with an assistant coach, demanding to be put back into a game his team was rallying from a sizable deficit to win and temporarily stave off elimination. "What did I tell you?" Michelle said after the story blew up and I called to give her a chance to gloat.

With the Thunder defeated, she could at least enjoy the rest of the playoffs without emotional investment. She was in awe of but didn't love LeBron James. She was astounded by the shooting dexterity of Stephen Curry, but since the Warriors' addition of Durant, they were *too* stacked a deck to root for. She liked the young players on Philadelphia and Boston but resented their ascension while her lousy Knicks were still promoting a roster reconstruction, a culture change they'd been promising since Dolan showed up to subvert it.

While trying to catch one game a week with Michelle, I found myself not as interested in watching at home, only checking in on the games for a few minutes before switching to cable news or going to sleep and catching up with the scores the next morning. I had always loved the playoffs dating back to high school and college, the Knicks' championship years, and certainly since my vocational attachment to the sport a few years later. But as the early rounds rolled by, I was distracted, disconnected. Beyond age catching up to me and having difficulty staying up late, the main reason was no great mystery.

By mid-May, the conference finals underway, I had not covered or attended a game, or written a word about the playoffs. Just as Michelle's years of official ticket ownership had ended with the current season, so, too, did it seem that my run of covering the playoffs—dating back to 1978—was over.

The *Times* was well stocked with smart coverage, having added Marc Stein, one of the premier NBA reporters in the country, to a staff that already included the very talented Scott Cacciola. I certainly had no right to be upset: The *Times* had treated me splendidly as a contributor after I had left the full-time staff in 2016, even sending me to the 2017 Finals in Oakland—albeit in a cramped coach middle seat where a young child positioned one row behind me passed the time kicking me in the back. So I wasn't dying to get on a plane to Cleveland, or anywhere, to rush into a crowded locker room, have television cameras crash into my skull, and swallow a diet of postgame clichés before facing another stressful deadline. But if I thought I had prepared myself for the eventuality of no longer being on the *Times* team, or any team, my mood gradually darkened as the playoffs continued. I found myself checking email, hoping to hear from an editor. Like Carmelo, I wanted back in—except I initially kept these thoughts to myself, not even mentioning them to Michelle.

That seemed only fair. Given her health issues, whatever problems I had were insignificant; it felt selfish to talk about myself. Calls to her now thus began with me trying to keep the conversation focused on how she was doing, or coping. She would play along for a few minutes, even admit that things weren't that great, but inevitably would change the subject to me. She couldn't help herself. With friends, this was just who Michelle was, her core identity: *being interested to be interesting.*

In all the time I had known her, I was aware of only one friend—a Greenwich businessman—who was so self-absorbed that Michelle made an abrupt decision to strike him from her life. I also intuitively trusted that our friendship at this point was beyond judgment, or risk. My resolve not to complain ultimately dissolved into admitting that not covering the playoffs had left me feeling a bit . . . empty. Detachment had begun to feel like disenfranchisement. Michelle wasted no time in getting on my case.

"So what you're telling me is that you're upset because you weren't invited to a party that you didn't want to go to anymore," she said.

"I guess I *thought* I didn't."

Fine, Michelle argued, we all want to be included in something, but doesn't everything get old? Hadn't I been complaining about the institutional repetition of covering sports? Hadn't I expressed a desire to connect elsewhere, do things I'd never had time for?

"Everything you've ever accomplished is visible in your clippings and on your bookshelf," she said. "You can see it and touch it—that's what I always thought was so great about being a journalist. And if that's not enough and you need to do it over and over again even if you don't have to, that means you're addicted to the drug of attention and that's pathetic."

Michelle's exasperation with me was nothing new—it was like a coach lacerating an underachieving star player for not hustling. But this sounded different. This was beyond irritation—more like anger.

"Michelle," I said, "are you upset?"

"Yes, I am," she said. "Because it makes me feel that I failed at my *job*. And because you've got time to try new things—and you don't want to be in the position to not have more time."

. . . .

My consecutive-years' playoff-coverage streak didn't end, after all. On a drive north to New England with Beth for a Memorial Day weekend getaway, an email dropped from a *Times* editor. A staffing emergency had arisen. Could I make it to Boston to cover Game 7 of the Celtics-Cavaliers Eastern Conference Finals on Sunday night of the holiday weekend?

Heading in the right direction, I leapt at the offer like a puppy whose dinner was hours overdue. I wrote a late-night deadline piece on another magnificent performance by LeBron James as he carried an otherwise pedestrian Cleveland team into a rematch of the three previous league Finals against Golden State.

Being at the game, reconnecting with several colleagues I hadn't seen all season, and catching up with the likes of the network announcers and old Knicks dignitaries Jeff Van Gundy and Mark Jackson was fun. But what really lifted my spirits was the next morning's feedback. While staying with relatives in a Boston suburb, I received texts and emails from colleagues. I appreciated that Michael Schmidt, who began his career in sports, took a moment from hounding Trump in the Washington bureau to weigh in with kind words about my tight-deadline work.

It was also painfully evident that Michelle was right. I had to admit that I still wanted attention, needed to be needed. I was the insecure guy found on Facebook by an old girlfriend and reassured that I still looked great. But was wanting a little applause every so often a sign of character weakness or just being human? I knew one thing: I felt good that morning—and reinvigorated enough to bang out yet another column for the Tuesday paper. And then I fired off a somewhat sheepish email to Michelle, with a link to my Game 7 piece:

OK, I TOOK THE DRUG AGAIN. TRYING TO WEAN MYSELF OFF. NOT THERE YET. WORKING AT IT.

Knowing Michelle, I figured she'd have a good laugh—tell me I was predictable, or pitiful, or both—but also assure me that she had enjoyed the column. She was, after all, my most faithful reader. But she didn't respond to the email on Monday, nor on Tuesday. When I called on Wednesday morning after arriving back home, she didn't seem to notice or recognize the 973 area code that always tipped her off that it was me. Instead of her usual "Hi, Harvey," she answered with her more official greeting from before caller ID: "Michelle Musler." Her voice was unsteady, halting. I knew right away: Something was wrong.

Usually when I asked Michelle how she was doing, she would make some offhand remark about "becoming dumb" but laugh it off when I pressed for more information and say, "Oh, I'm fine." This time there was no *but*, no laugh, no acknowledgment of columns I had written or the email I had sent. She just said, "I've been better."

She explained that she had suffered another seizure, the first she had mentioned—at least to me—in a while, after an adjustment had been made to her medication. She had fallen on the stairs of her condo in the early morning while experiencing what she called a hallucination—she had imagined Robin Kelly was in the house, calling to her from downstairs. She admitted that she had for the past few weeks been making more regular visits to her neurologist for increased observation and testing.

"There are some things going on," she said. "Just not ready to talk about it yet."

"Michelle," I said, "you're scaring me."

She offered nothing specific, only that she had more tests scheduled.

"Have you told the family?"

"No, I haven't," she said. "Because there's nothing to tell them yet and nothing they can do."

"What can I do?"

"Nothing," she said. I'd be among the first to know when there was more definitive news.

I called every day for the remainder of the week, trying to pry more information from her. She wanted only to talk about the Finals, specifically the Cavaliers' J. R. Smith's incredible mental lapse in Game 1: He had forgotten that the score was tied and dribbled out the final seconds of regulation without taking a shot. The Cavaliers went on to lose in overtime. "The look on LeBron's face was priceless," she said.

On the morning after Game 2, she told me that she was struggling to follow the action and to determine which team was scoring. The colors of the uniforms were confusing her. "But I'm still enjoying it tremendously," she said. "One of the plays made by Durant caused me to nearly jump out of my seat."

"How about I come up and watch a game with you?" I said.

"I'd love that," she said. "But you'd better come soon."

. . . .

The day before Game 3, on the afternoon of Tuesday, June 5, Michelle finally broke the horrible news: She had what appeared to be a malignant mass in her lung—and her doctors feared that the cancer had spread to her brain. Hearing this news was a punch to the gut, leaving me in a near-speechless state of disbelief.

"When they showed me the report all I saw was *malignancy*," she said. "It threw me into a tizzy. I told them, 'This is pretty fast—I thought I was being treated for strokes.'"

But how could this be? How long had she known? Her memory was fuzzy, but I gathered from what she was saying that the first suspicious scans had been seen sometime in May. In cases of lung cancer, she'd been told that detection was often delayed until advanced stages. Metastasis could be swift, and lethal.

I did the quick calculation and realized that she had to have known *something* serious was afoot when I complained to her on the phone about not covering the playoffs just before Memorial Day weekend. So she hadn't been speaking generally about making better use of time. She had to already have known that hers was running short.

I swallowed hard, took a deep breath, felt the tears come.

"Michelle, I'm so . . . sorry."

"Well, I'm almost eighty-two years old—something was bound to get me," she said.

What could I do? When could I come see her? She wasn't sure. She was facing more consultations, more tests. The official confirmation of the two malignancies was made early the following week. The prognosis was dire. The family had to be notified. Brandon, who lived the closest of her five children, quickly arrived from Manhattan to stay with Michelle at her condo and help sort out a plan. The others began making travel arrangements to join him.

On the phone, in brief conversations, Michelle shifted between disorientation and clearheadedness, saying she had lost track of time but bragging to me the day after Game 3 that she had outlasted Brandon, who had fallen asleep before the Warriors won for a third straight time. Her obsession with the Finals at first sounded a little crazy, but upon reflection, it was quite remarkable, if not altogether unpredictable. Michelle's life had taken the most terrifying of turns, and yet a basketball game could still be her anchor in the storm. It could momentarily distract—or anesthetize—her from the fear.

Trivial as it seemed, she still wanted to talk about the game when I called. But if that was what she wanted—and needed—why not? I asked her what she thought of the highlight-reel pass LeBron had thrown to himself off the backboard for a dunk. "That was in the first quarter when everything still looked good for Cleveland," she said without missing a beat.

For Michelle's sake, I suddenly found myself hoping the series would go the distance, seven games, but the Warriors were by far the better team, and it seemed likely to end as soon as the following night. Brandon told me I was welcome to come up and watch what was likely to be the last game with them. I initially said I would but thought better of it; I was hesitant to be in the way of precious family time.

Instead, I reached out to Michelle's friends, knowing that her children, arriving from points west, north, and south, would be preoccupied with their mother. Ernestine Miller. Lori Hamamoto. A few others. They—we—all were in shock, wondering how her doctors could have missed a mass in her lung and helpless to do anything but hope there would still be time to see her.

Several days later, after Michelle had been admitted to Stamford Hospital, I knocked on the door to her room and walked in. It was midafternoon. She was sitting up in bed. Only one other person was with her, a young woman by her side. I hesitated and offered to come back, but Michelle, her face brightening, told me it was fine to stay. I soon realized that I had arrived at a delicate moment, in the middle of a session with a hospital psychologist. They seemed to be reflecting on Michelle's life—her five children, her many friends, her work, and of course her long love affair with the Knicks. She nodded toward me and said, "I have this wonderful friend because of it."

"It sounds like you have *many* people who care about you and that you've had a very fulfilling life," the psychologist said.

"Oh, absolutely," Michelle said. "No complaints."

The dual kindness and cruelty of their conversation hit me at that moment. I was witnessing the brave confrontation of a terminal situation. Michelle knew she was going to die, though without a real sense of how much time she had left. Alone for the next couple of hours, we avoided the subject—more because I just wasn't yet ready to go there. We talked about normal stuff: The end of the NBA season. The mess in Washington. Her kids. My kids. Her grandkids. She told me how relieved she was that her artistic granddaughter, Dylan, had decided not to quit a good job in Manhattan for what sounded like a quixotic adventure with a boyfriend in Italy. Through it all, she was in good spirits, alert except for one brief period when she dozed off. Concerned that it might be more than fatigue, I raised my voice. She opened her eyes.

"Michelle, am I boring you?"

"Never," she said.

When the staff called to take her dinner order, she requested a Caesar salad, steak bits, sweet potato *and* sweet potato fries, and rice pudding for dessert. She ate almost everything—reassuring me for the moment that she was still strong.

I told her that friends were asking to see her, but she demurred. She made a point of saying that she didn't want to put Lori out by making her come all the way from Washington. Even now, she hated the thought of being fussed over or, worse, pitied. Whatever there was to say could be said by phone.

"So you're telling me that if anyone else comes to visit you won't let them in?"

"Oh, you know what I mean," she said, smirking.

I did. Michelle just wanted me to know that she would not be insulted if people didn't come, but I also knew that she would be happy to see whoever showed up. So I returned a few days later with Jay Greenberg, another of her sportswriting pals.

Their friendship, like so many others, had begun at the Garden; Michelle had seen to it. Jay was a newcomer to the *New York Post* column lineup in 1994, best known in Philadelphia for a hockey expertise that eventually landed him in that sport's Hall of Fame. Suddenly he was covering Pat Riley's Knicks on the way to the NBA Finals, uncertain he was up to the challenge of a much less familiar sport at a moment when interest in the team had soared. A woman stepped forward from the front row near the Knicks bench one night, gave him an unsolicited pat on the back. "I'm enjoying your columns," Michelle told him. He was surprised she even knew him, but happily accepted the praise. He came from a family of non–sports fans and in that respect, Michelle became for Jay what she had long been for me—the familiar and comforting face in the amorphous collective otherwise known as his readership.

Jay and I met in the hospital lobby. On the way to her room, he asked me how Michelle had seemed when I had visited her last, what he might expect. "Actually, she was OK," I said. But she was much less than that this time. It was obvious from the moment we sat down on opposite sides of the bed that the cancer was wasting no time. Her voice was weaker, scratchier. Her face had less color. She wasn't very talkative, though she listened attentively and laughed along as Jay and I swapped newspaper war stories.

A doctor came by, telling Michelle that he and the staff were checking scans, trying to determine what the next steps might be.

"Steps?" she said. "No more steps."

Michelle had obviously moved on from being "in a tizzy." She was in the full-acceptance stage and made this exceedingly clear as we stood up to leave upon hearing that a couple of her children were on their way and she wouldn't be alone for very long.

"I'll see you again, Michelle," Jay told her as he stepped toward the door.

Michelle shook her head.

"I hope not," she said.

I will admit that my next visit with Michelle was timed with an ulterior motive. I was hoping we could share one more event, make one last basketball memory. It was June 21, the night of the annual NBA draft, long a staple of both our calendars. She wouldn't miss it if she knew it was on. But I had driven to Stamford forewarned by her children that Michelle's deterioration had been swift. She was past the point of wanting to be seen, insisting on phone farewells with friends instead. I was relieved to be told by her children that her door remained open to me.

It was dinnertime when I arrived. Michelle's daughter Devon was trying to entice her with small pieces of meat and roasted potatoes. Less than two weeks after her small feast, Michelle would submit to only an occasional half-hearted bite, preferring to sip water through a straw in a cup I held to her mouth.

About an hour passed. I checked my phone. It was nearly seven, the draft's start time. I wasn't sure if I should suggest that we turn on the television, or if I should even stay much longer, never quite knowing if I was intruding on time with her children. But Devon was fatigued and emotionally spent after a long afternoon. What the hell, I decided—why not ask?

"Oh, is that tonight?" Michelle said.

"In a few minutes," I told her.

"Oh, yes," she said, pointing to the screen on the wall. Suddenly perked up, she asked for the back of her bed to be raised and for pillows to be propped. Knowing her mother would be preoccupied with the draft until it was time to sleep, Devon left for the short drive to Michelle's condo.

Michelle was actually never much of a college basketball fan, but she, like many followers of the NBA, loved the draft because of its reality-TV pageantry—the family group hugs that signified the realization of a dream and imminent wealth. On draft night, she could also harbor the never-ending and never-fulfilled hope that the Knicks would finally land *their* Michael Jordan, *their* LeBron James. But that wasn't likely in 2018, with the team holding the ninth pick in the first round. We watched mostly in silence as the first players were chosen and made their triumphant strolls to the stage for the ceremonial donning of the team cap and the photo-op shaking of Commissioner Adam Silver's hand. The names rattled off—Deandre Ayton, Marvin Bagley, Luka Doncic. Michelle watched quietly as the video highlights for each player were shown and the analysts dissected their games.

Finally, the Knicks were on a five-minute clock between picks. She watched intently as the announcers reviewed the Knicks' season and their most glaring needs. She nodded when I said, "They need everything." And she added, for good measure, "New ownership."

Out came Silver to announce, "With the ninth pick in the 2018 NBA draft, the New York Knicks select . . . Kevin Knox of the University of Kentucky." There were jeers in the crowd at Brooklyn's Barclays Center. One announcer pointed out that the fans had also booed Kristaps Porzingis on draft night in 2015. Another was dismayed that people would treat an eighteen-year-old so rudely in the biggest moment of his life.

"Idiots," Michelle said.

"You got that right," I said.

"And the players from Kentucky," she said, "don't they usually turn out to be pretty good?"

"They do, but he's a baby, like most of these guys," I said. "Probably take him a few years."

"Good," she said. "Then I won't miss anything when I'm not around next season."

I let her gallows humor pass without comment, knowing Michelle would never abide a half-hearted reassurance. We watched the next few selections in silence—which made me reflect on how rare an occurrence it was in nearly four decades of a friendship that had in effect been one continuous conversation. Her eyelids were getting heavy, the adrenaline rush provided by the wait for the Knicks' pick fading fast. With the assistance of morphine, Michelle wasn't in pain—at least her doctors had assured her children of that much. But I didn't want her to stave off sleep on my account. I knew I couldn't stay much longer. But there was one question that I needed to ask. One last thing I had to know.

"Michelle, are you OK?"

I assumed she knew by the pained sound of my voice that I was not asking if she was merely comfortable, free of pain. Perhaps selfishly, I wanted to know what this remarkable woman who had taught me so much about living was thinking about dying.

She nodded. "I'm OK," she said softly. "I'm really OK."

That was all she would volunteer, and it would have to be enough to convince me that Michelle indeed was ready, that she was at peace because she believed her world was in order.

"How are *you* feeling?" she said.

"I'm sad, but I'm OK, too."

"You should be OK," she said. "You have a great life."

"You know that you helped a lot with that, Michelle," I said. "Thank you."

"Thank *you* for letting me," she said.

I wanted to say so much more but her eyes were losing the struggle to stay open, while mine filled with tears. It was time for her to sleep, and for me to leave. I stood up, leaned over to kiss her cheek. With night falling outside, the room was darkened, the only light flickering from the television screen. I moved toward the door and took a look back. Michelle's eyes were closed.

"Love you, Michelle."

"Love you, Harvey."

I stepped out of the room and closed the door on a precious friendship, the likes of which I knew I would never have again.

Twelve

The Postseason

Michelle Musler died on the afternoon of June 28, almost two months before her eighty-second birthday. An email from her daughter Darcy dropped with the news at 6:28 that evening, the subject line reading, simply: "Mom."

HI HARVEY, YOU ARE THE FIRST FRIEND I AM REACHING OUT TO FOR OUR FAMILY. MICHELLE PASSED THIS AFTERNOON . . . WE ALL GOT THE LOVELY CHANCE TO THANK HER AND TELL HER HOW SHE SHAPED AND MOLDED US. WE THINK SHE DIDN'T SUFFER AND ALL TRIED TO MAKE HER END OF LIFE MEANINGFUL AND PEACEFUL. XXOO. DARCY.

I read the email, took a deep breath, and let the tears come again. I read it a second time but when the finality of it all had set in, I somehow found myself amusingly struck by Michelle's strategically impeccable timing: A true NBA fan, she fought off death right through the Finals and the draft. Yes, she would miss the annual July splash of free-agency signings, but the most significant one—LeBron James to the Lakers—had been no great mystery to her, or anyone who remained in the world of the living.

For those of us who loved Michelle, and certainly for me, her life's conclusion was a bitter pill but one made more acceptable by the gentle ambience of her final days. My father had died in 1990 of sudden heart failure, leaving so much hauntingly unspoken, unresolved. Not so with Michelle. Her thunderclap diagnosis of cancer and subsequent demise were stunningly swift but not enough to prevent all of us—by bedside or phone—to say good-bye in whatever way we needed to say it.

Most important, there was enough time for her children to gather round her while she was alert, communicative, and largely still herself. To tell her things—as Darcy confided and her other children would later confirm—that I knew better than anyone she had longed to hear. Outside her hospital room, her daughter Devon had sobbed when I shared the maternal misgivings Michelle had expressed to me in the final months of her life. Yes, of course there had been issues, she said, and there was emotional scar tissue. But certainly in adulthood it was soothed by appreciation and respect for the enormous challenges her mother had met. As Blair, the youngest of the five children, said when I repeated what I had told Devon, "She was the one who stayed!"

Though Michelle never did relinquish the hope for more quality time, more days preoccupied with newspapers and yoga, NBA games in high definition, and even the occasional return to her courtside haven, I did believe she was *really OK*, or at worst relieved that there would be no prolonged, futile struggle with dementia after all—no plunge into what she imagined as nursing home hell and no drawn-out time of being a burden to anyone, especially her children. That was the fate she had dreaded more than death: becoming a drain on their lives. It was why she had sacrificed considerable annual sums that challenged her retirement budget from late middle age to buy a long-term health-care policy that would have provided nursing care had she needed it.

She was far from broke, though, and in those final days, she told me how grateful she was that her children would inherit the remains of her estate. Divided by five, it would amount to nothing life-changing, but it was a fortification of her parental claim as the provider—the one her children could count on.

Unproductive as grudge-holding was—at least that was what Michelle had long lectured me—I knew that she held onto the ire caused by her failed marriage and the ensuing financial hardship, apparently right to the end. Presumed to be unconscious by her children during one of her final days, she startled them by cursing her ex when she had apparently overheard them mention him. In adulthood, all of her children could easily imagine how difficult and frightening those early years must have been for Michelle—far more easily than when they were young, dealing with their own needs and fears. How could there not be some resentment, even when they could intellectualize her sacrifices— or, once Michelle had reconstructed her work and social life, the time she had *not* sacrificed for them? While her sons had married and had children, her three daughters had not. Michelle did occasionally wonder if the example she and her ex had set had soured them on the institution.

In adulthood, Darcy was by her own admission the most

distant of Michelle's children, though her corporate work was most similar to her mother's. Years passed between visits to Stamford from the West Coast. Yet Michelle was over the moon when Darcy, after being downsized out of a corporate position during the Great Recession, didn't wallow in misfortune, picked herself up in 2009, and redirected her life, as Michelle had once done. She headed abroad for several years to Russia and Turkey to teach English, a reinvention of which Michelle was proud.

"I've always thought that maybe we butted heads so much because she was the one most like me," Michelle told me, while accepting her share of the blame—she could be overly judgmental and critical of life or career decisions, and was especially cool upon learning of Darcy's early career decision to work with her father. Their relationship, perhaps more so than the others, took measure of the complexity one would expect from a large family having come through such domestic upheaval—and one ultimately scattered around a large country, their time together growing more infrequent in later years, perhaps making it harder and harder to say the things that needed to be said.

Minor familial tensions persisted even in Michelle's final months. In the late summer of 2017, she had invited Blair to come east from Los Angeles for the last weekend of the US Open. Blair preferred a one-stop arrangement that would require fewer accumulated miles. Michelle nagged her to splurge on a nonstop flight, arguing that there could be delays or cancellations and their weekend watching tennis would be marred, or ruined. What she really meant to say—and what she told me—was: *I may never see you again, and I don't want anything to get screwed up!*

In Devon's case, having long since relocated to Florida, she had not seen her mother in several years when she walked into her hospital room and heard a familiar refrain: "Are you going to do something with your hair?" It was Michelle's corporatist complaint to her bohemian daughter, an annoyance Devon had braced herself for on many a visit to Connecticut. This time, she blurted out her final declaration of independence: "No, I'm not!" Mother and daughter finally had a hearty laugh about something they would never agree on.

From her more enlightened perch, and with her mother on her deathbed, Devon could accept the cons with the pros, Michelle in full. She evaluated her mother as a "kind of martyr . . . a Hester Prynne" of the Connecticut suburbs, "forward-thinking for her time, a bold woman living in a man's world." Whatever resentments lingered—such as Brandon's suspicion that the family's Connecticut summer home had been sold off in part to support Michelle's basketball habit—all of the Musler siblings accepted and admired the unlikely life she had willed herself into. Against gender and cultural odds, a suburban mother of five had made herself at home in a world whose stars were largely young black men from inner cities. The evidence of her social standing had long ago taken up residence in the family albums they had perused at Michelle's condo during her final days—snapshots in time that were clearly not contrived fan-photo ops.

One evening during the final days, her kids and I reminisced over beers on Michelle's back patio, and someone asked if I had been aware that she had actually once dated a retired Knick. I didn't have a clue, and was initially astonished and even a little hurt by this rare piece of basketball gossip Michelle had not shared. But back in the day, she never did reveal much about whatever romantic interests she'd had. Maybe it was our age difference, our sometime parent-child dynamic, a need for limits and privacy. But the more I thought about it, it also made sense to me that she had dated someone inside the basketball bubble, given how much time and effort she had invested there. And why begrudge her that after all she'd been through, Devon said. Having expunged her adolescent musings of whether Michelle loved the Knicks and the whole Garden scene more than anything, including her children, why shouldn't Michelle have had the chance to be different, "to enjoy being *her*"?

In a rare display of self-pity, Michelle once admitted to me, during the earliest days of her decline, that if she managed to live long enough, there might not be a half dozen people beyond her family left to attend her funeral because so many she had known had already passed. But a month after she died, Michelle's children staged a beautiful celebration of life at a Stamford hotel event room that was crowded with her family and friends.

Brandon was the host and introductory speaker, providing loving context to Michelle's life, referring to, without going into specific detail, the uncommon challenges most of the guests were still not privy to. Then he tagged me—without advance notice, an apparent oversight in the rush of planning—as the next speaker. As I hesitatingly made my way forward, I had no written text, no Michelle-inspired bullet points, no planned or resolute idea of what I would actually say.

I looked out at the audience, Michelle's children and grandchildren, her friends—including Lori Hamamoto and Ernestine Miller, Jay Greenberg and Wynn Plaut—whom I knew and those I did not. One spontaneous, wishful thought thankfully came to mind. I said that if I could have five more precious minutes on the phone with Michelle, what I would most want to tell her—and what I was sure she would be dying to hear—was that I had written her obituary in the *New York Times*.

It was the most precious of tributes I could give her, but I have to give credit where it's due: Ernestine Miller was the first one to suggest that I try. I reminded her that *Times* obits were generally reserved for people who wrote bestselling novels and cured mysterious diseases. Much to my surprise, and delight, Bill McDonald, the obits editor, responded to my pitch—the woman behind the Knicks bench for forty-plus years—within minutes. "Sure, who wouldn't read that?" he said.

Urgently reporting as I would for a breaking story, I phoned the always-approachable Jeff Van Gundy. We chatted for a while before I got to the point. "Jeff, when you coached in New York, there was a woman who sat behind the bench—"

"You mean Michelle?" he interrupted.

In the time since Van Gundy had left the Garden in 2001, he no doubt had engaged countless people around the country, faces he had to recognize, names he needed to remember. Yet Michelle's was still at the tip of his tongue, which told me that she had been as much a fixture at the Garden as any player, coach, or employee. I had hoped for some color for the piece, and he did not disappoint:

"Whenever I would walk out on the floor, disheveled with my collar up or my tie crooked, she would come up from behind, fix it, and just step back to her seat with a smile but without saying a word," Van Gundy said.

With that one quote, Van Gundy captured the essence of Michelle's decades behind the bench: her desire and ability to meaningfully connect, make her presence felt without making a scene. Alongside the full obituary ran a beautiful color photograph of her, dressed all in black, standing by her row, with Wynn Plaut a few feet behind her, graciously ceding the spotlight.

Of course, nowhere in the piece was it mentioned that Michelle had been *my* career coach, courtside source, and so much more. The truth was, I had straddled or crossed a fine professional line by even pitching her obit, given our close friendship. But she had so loved newspapers, particularly the *Times*. In one of the photos her children had used for a slideshow at her celebration of life, the camera had lovingly captured her in her courtside seat, from behind, peering down at the front sports page of the *Times*—her pregame routine until her friends and fans made their way over.

In the last months of her life, as I made my weekly visits to Stamford, I couldn't help but notice the stacks of newspapers— particularly the *Times*—grow higher and higher. I asked her one night if she was planning on lining a few hundred birdcages with all the excess paper. She laughed ruefully. "It takes me forever to get through one day's worth," she said. "But if I don't, then I feel like I'm failing at keeping up."

In a snowballing era of trashy clickbait, lightweight sites, and outright fakery, she was allergic to news online, steadfastly oldschool. Only print that rubbed off on her fingers represented legitimacy and gravitas. Above all news sources, to be on those gray pages of the *Times* was to *matter*, to have made it—if not for the sake of fame, then for a sense of self-actualization.

Michelle, like me, was proud of what she had achieved against the odds. On the day her obit was posted on the *Times*'s website, I had a flashback to one of the things she had told me about being afraid to let go of my work—it was all right there, in the archives, for me to reconnect with, to reassure myself of what I had done. What joy I felt in knowing that her extraordinary life—if only in roughly nine hundred words—was now there as well, and would be forever.

The response to Michelle's obituary was swift and widespread. The Knicks public relations staff inquired about a family contact, wanting to offer an expression of sympathy. Many who knew her from the Garden emailed their memories, heartfelt and whimsical alike. Steffi Berne, who sat behind Michelle with her husband, Bob, affectionately wrote in an email that she would never forget the night Michelle read her the riot act for having the audacity to unfold a newspaper *during* a game, which she insisted was disrespectful to the players. Tim Walsh, a former Knicks trainer, fondly recalled Michelle's knack for sending a note of congratulations or sympathy whenever she would hear he had started or lost another job—making the point that she didn't forget people after they'd moved on.

One Garden employee emailed to say that he had watched Michelle more than hold her own with high-powered men who had the mistaken idea they could sweet-talk her into a swindle in the ongoing resale ticket exchange that courtside fans typically engaged in. "You couldn't get anything past her," said the employee, requesting anonymity in deference to James Dolan's media policies. And then there was Charles Oakley, by reputation the fiercest and most candid of all the Knicks, who understood how tough-minded Michelle must have been just to be in her seat— night after night, season after season—while juggling all of life's obligations.

"The Oak Man of Knicks fans," he called her when I reached him by phone.

And why was that?

"People, you know, they appreciated me for how I played, sacrificed my body," he said. "Michelle better than anyone knew that no one ever had to get on me to play hard because she was sitting right there and heard everything. Just like me, she was there every night for over forty years, all the way from Connecticut, two hours in and two hours out, and after all the operations she had on her knee, her back. She was a warrior. Everybody always makes a big deal about Spike, but he comes in a chauffeured car from the Upper East Side—you know what I'm saying?"

I did. And when he said it I could have kicked myself for not having called him sooner. In the obituary, I had quoted Lori Hamamoto calling Michelle "as big a staple at the Garden as Spike Lee." It was a splendid line, but Oakley's quote was richer, even, than Van Gundy's. While he was always colorful and occasionally controversial, he was rarely off the mark. "The Oak Man of Knicks fans" was a classic and fitting tribute. And there were still more to come.

O n opening night of the 2018–19 NBA season, when even a team pegged to be one of the worst in the league could play dress-up and pretend to be elite, the Knicks acknowledged neither extreme. They merely cast themselves as a franchise with heart and loyal fans. Each one in attendance was greeted with a souvenir T-shirt draped over the back of their seat. It was Knicks blue with an orange team logo, the name of the obligatory bank sponsor, and an inscription in white lettering: "New York Forever." The ambiguous marketing slogan suggested only that better times were coming at some future date while promising nothing for the present.

Meanwhile, behind the Knicks bench, in the first row of section 6, on seat 13, sat a token of appreciation for an important part of the dearly departed past. It was a colorful bouquet of flowers—in memoriam, for Michelle, who had never abandoned her team, through good times, bad times, and, more recently, horrendous times. A security guard kept vigil. His mission was to ensure that they remained on the seat Michelle had long occupied until the season tip-off against the Atlanta Hawks.

I had come to the Garden that night having asked to write a curtain-raising column for the *Times*, but with an ulterior motive. I had to be there in the event the Knicks' public relations staff followed up on its stated summer promise of "wanting to do something" for Michelle. The team had already contributed in her name to a Stamford library, but the flowers constituted a more public statement.

As much of a turnoff as James Dolan's Knicks had been over the previous two decades, I had to admit to being moved by the gesture. I didn't kid myself that he—more likely to eject a fan than fete one—was so much as aware of it. But during the pregame period, as the players casually launched shots at the basket and Garden regulars greeted one another like it was the first day of school, I hung with the security guard, explaining to the occasional inquirer what, or whom, they were for. "The best Knicks fan ever," was my standard line.

Not everyone had to ask. Mike Breen took a few moments from his broadcast preparation to comment on how kind Michelle could be, how she often asked about his family or complimented him on his suit or his work on the MSG Network with Walt Frazier.

"The last ten years she would say, 'This might be my last,' but you just knew she wasn't going anywhere," Breen said. "She loved it so much, and I always said it was people like Michelle who make the NBA so great, who give an arena its character, more so than in any other sport. Because they're so close, they can literally reach out and touch you and create that special bond."

As if to validate his longtime partner's point, Frazier strolled by—in one of his trademark loud sports jackets that looked like it had been lifted from the wall of a modern art museum—to second the motion that Michelle was among the very special people at the Garden. He recalled ribbing her endlessly about having never patronized his far–West Side restaurant, until she arranged a year-end School of Visual Arts staff party that was at that point the joint's largest booking. I wondered what her reaction would have been to the tributes she was getting on this night—especially from someone like the iconic Clyde. Embarrassed? Flattered? Probably both.

With game time approaching and fans streaming in, the security guard removed the flowers from seat 13, whose occupant for this night and many more to come would be Noah Goodhart. I vaguely remembered Goodhart from the game I had attended with Michelle early during the previous season against Brooklyn. She had thanked him by name after he delivered a bottle of water to her from the club before the start of the second half, as he apparently did many nights after it became a struggle for Michelle to navigate the crowd.

Young. Rich. Scooping up the best seats in the house. On the surface, Goodhart seemed like the kind of replacement fan Michelle used to say she would cringe upon seeing in her seat when she tuned in on TV. Noah and Jonah Goodhart had for some time been buying Michelle's other seats, on the railing. The brothers eventually suggested partnering with Plaut on the seats directly behind the bench after he purchased his Florida home.

But the Goodhart brothers, more than casual fans, were actual basketball junkies, sons of modest-earning educators in Ann Arbor, Michigan. During the Bad Boys era of the Detroit Pistons, they attended games with freebie tickets supplied by local businesses. They sat at the top of the Pontiac Silverdome, their view obstructed by a giant curtain cutting off half the massive football stadium in a futile attempt to create an intimacy more conducive to basketball. The brothers wound up in New York, starting, running, and investing in internet companies, amassing a fortune. To Michelle, their backstory as self-made men made the difference. They were legitimate fans, not rich kids handed their status in life or stargazers in search of a hot scene.

Soon the players were introduced. The national anthem was sung. The season tipped off. Just before halftime, as the Knicks blitzed Atlanta with forty-nine points in the second quarter—the highest-scoring quarter in franchise history—I received a slew of text messages. Breen and Frazier—as they had indicated to me before the game they would—had paid tribute to Michelle on the MSG Network broadcast. On the train home that night, I emailed a photo I had taken of the flowers to Michelle's children and told them that while she was gone from the Garden, she was not forgotten. There was also evidence in the arena that she never would be.

Following their opening-night victory, the young Knicks reverted to predicted form, dropping five of their next six games. On Halloween night, they hosted the Indiana Pacers in a rare nationally televised appearance on ESPN, which brought Van Gundy back to town. Early in the game, he took the opportunity to make a nationally televised homage to Michelle, a recounting of the clothes-grooming story he had shared with me months earlier for the obit. He also mentioned a ninety-five-dollar playoff ticket of Michelle's that was on display in the Garden.

Actually, there were two: one from Game 2 of the 1993 Eastern Conference Finals, featuring John Starks's dunk on Horace Grant and Michael Jordan, and a second from a 1999 conference finals playoff game, which the Knicks had won on Larry Johnson's miracle four-point play (a three-point shot and accompanying foul) against the Larry Bird–coached Pacers.

For a team without a championship in decades, these were cherished moments that Jonathan Supranowitz, the former PR director, had set out to memorialize when the Garden was renovated. On the prowl for souvenirs, he asked Michelle if she had anything left from her most savored games. She showed up early for the next game, carrying a Tupperware container filled with tickets from every Garden playoff game she had ever attended. "Help yourself," she said. Her Starks and Johnson tickets were encased and hung in separate concourses along with the famous photos, the players' jerseys, and plaques that acknowledged the donors. "Her name will be on those walls for as long as they are up," Supranowitz told me not long after Michelle had died.

On opening night, I went looking for the Starks dunk exhibit and found it a short walk from the media workroom, on the Garden's sixth level. I snapped a photo and stood there awhile, relishing the sight of Michelle's name etched in Knicks history. Short of having her actual seat number retired and hung high in the Garden rafters, what more could any forever fan want?

Postscript

Dear Michelle:

The 2018–19 NBA season had its interesting moments, leading to a wild, rousing finish, but to be honest, for me it ultimately fell flat, like trying to dribble a ball rapidly leaking air. That's because after nearly forty years, you weren't around to share it with. And I know what you would tell me: *Grow up. Move on.* I'm working at that, but life hasn't been quite the same without you, my life coach and special friend.

Beth tells me that I have seemed particularly melancholy on Sundays—our phone catch-up day—wandering around the house after the morning news shows as if I was supposed to be doing *something*, trying to remember exactly what it was. So I'm hoping that writing these words will compensate for what has gone unsaid—though I must tell you right from the top that the less said about the 2018–19 Knicks, the better! More on that later.

I should begin with something I know will make your day. Not that you were one to celebrate the misfortune of others, but we both know how little use you had for Carmelo Anthony. So it seems that his chronic self-absorption finally caught up with him. Sick of his act after one season, the

Thunder shipped him to the Rockets in Houston soon after you left us. That deal raised a whole lot of eyebrows, since it meant a reunion with Mike D'Antoni.

It was one of those overhyped NBA transactions—the aging Melo teaming up with Chris Paul and James Harden to create another so-called Big 3. D'Antoni bit his lip and insisted that what had happened in New York was long forgotten. Melo claimed he was at the point in his career that he could play for anybody. And then their remarriage lasted exactly . . . ten games! The fact that Paul, Melo's good buddy and the outspoken president of the players' union, apparently didn't vouch for him or utter one public word in protest after the Rockets basically told him to just go home is all I—and you—need to know. So go ahead, Michelle, pour yourself a heavenly glass of wine. I'll toast your instincts from here.

Speaking of purging and prophecies, I emailed Blair to ask what *did* ever happen to your condo-ful of Knicks memorabilia—which you, of course, predicted many times would be deposited in the trash soon after you were gone. She responded that each of the kids took a T-shirt and her dear friend Zander Lane made off with a bobblehead. "That's about it," she wrote. "However, on the bright side, I can hear Mom saying (almost as if she's standing next to me), *you mean I got something right?* She said we'd toss it and we did. I know she'd rather be right any day than have us keep all her Knicks stuff."

So, congratulations on that, Michelle, but you also should know that your children held a beautiful celebration of your life and there was no shortage of guests—so that prediction you got totally wrong! You were loved by so many. You are missed. Blair also saved and shared with her siblings—and me!—many of your Christmas letters, dating back to the midsixties. Reading your annual life updates and tributes to your children, I don't know how anybody could have ever questioned your devotion to them. Your letters were so well written, so sweet yet sardonic. They reminded me of how you wanted to be a journalist—and had you been born twenty-five years later, there is no doubt in my mind that *you* could have been Selena Roberts, the first woman to have written Sports of the Times.

Speaking of which, I have continued contributing the occasional column or story for the *Times*, though opening night was the only night I attended a Knicks game during the entire 2018–19 season—and that was because I correctly suspected that the Knicks PR staff would do the right thing and honor you, with a bouquet of flowers that was left on your seat until game time. Outside of that night, though— and as you suspected when we watched the draft from your hospital room the last time I visited—you didn't miss a damn thing. The 2018–19 Knicks won seventeen games, tying for the worst franchise record with the team Phil Jackson ran as president in 2014–15. Imagine paying a thousand dollars a night for that! (Wynn, ensconced in Florida, told me he only went to one game and had more or less ceded the tickets to the Goodhart brothers.)

OK, I *really* buried the lede because I didn't want to begin with news that I know would have had you spitting venom. Not only did Kristaps Porzingis fail to return from his knee injury, but the Knicks shocked everyone early in the New

Year by trading him to Dallas, along with a few overpaid players to clear enough salary cap space to sign two premier free agents from the 2019 summer class.

Throughout the season, all we heard was that Kevin Durant would leave the Warriors for the Knicks and that Kyrie Irving would walk out on the Celtics in July 2019 to partner with him in New York—along with whichever stud college player the Knicks would extract from the draft. Instant championship contender!

The college player Knicks fans were fixated on was Zion Williamson, a one-and-done sensation from Duke, said to be a generational talent, just like LeBron. So, yes, another much-ballyhooed Knicks plan to organically build a team around Porzingis was scrapped in the pursuit of a get-rich-quick infusion of superstar talent their front office— including James Dolan—was practically guaranteeing.

Then the draft lottery concluded with the Knicks among the last four teams standing and the one with the best statistical chance to land the number one pick. For a few minutes, or until the end of the commercial break, it was all happening! Then the pick went to New Orleans. The Knicks finished third, which deflated the fan base until it realized that R. J. Barrett, Williamson's college teammate, had been the top-ranked high school player of that class and promised to be much more than a consolation prize. So hopes remained high. Free agency was coming—along with Irving and Durant.

But as you often and so eloquently put it: *Everything at the Garden always turns to shit.* Durant ruptured an Achilles tendon in the Finals (helping Toronto win a thrilling championship during what amounted to a one-season rental of Kawhi Leonard) over the Warriors. Durant and Irving did, in fact, decide to team up in New York—but it was in Brooklyn, with the Nets, who had made the playoffs with a talented young nucleus. As we always said, build a culture and the stars will come.

I couldn't help but channel what I imagined your reaction to all of this would have been into the column the *Times* asked me to write. At the risk of sounding shrill, I excoriated Dolan for blighting the Garden's curb appeal with his disrespect of fans and bad body language. In a landmark summer for superstar movement, none of them chose or so much as took a meeting with the loser Knicks. Kawhi bolted from Toronto and landed in Los Angeles with the Clippers—joined there by Paul George, who had asked for a trade from Oklahoma City. That left your guy, Russell Westbrook, as the lone Thunder star, but not for long. He was traded to Houston to reunite with James Harden, in a deal for Chris Paul and draft picks. Anthony Davis strong-armed his way out of New Orleans and went to the Lakers to join LeBron. A humbled Carmelo even resurfaced early in the 2019–20 season with Portland.

Then the retired commissioner, David Stern, died at seventy-seven on the very day the calendar flipped ominously to 2020, weeks after he'd suffered a brain hemorrhage. Soon after that came an unspeakable tragedy mourned worldwide: Kobe Bryant, his thirteen-year-old daughter, and seven others were killed in a helicopter crash. And finally, horrifically, the world (as we knew it) ended. The 2019–20 NBA season shut down in March along with the rest of sports, the country, and much of the planet when a contagious and deadly virus struck China, spread into Europe, and surged into the United States and New York, to the point where the metropolitan area became the pandemic's epicenter. The virus killed hundreds of thousands of people worldwide and especially struck the elderly. We hunkered down at home, distanced socially from loved ones, wary of even stepping into a market. I'm truly grateful that you didn't have to live through this nightmare, but of course in such terrifying times I missed you more than ever.

Backtracking, I should tell you that around the 2018 Christmas holidays, I visited again with our pal Patrick at Georgetown, this time for a story on him coaching Alonzo Mourning's son. By coincidence, I got there the day after Lori had resigned as the basketball team's PR person for a job in New York. Helping me with my story was her last order of business, which seemed fitting, she said. But Lori being loyal Lori, she also felt guilty about abandoning her buddy Patrick after half of a second season for a higher-paying position in New York. In the role of surrogate Michelle, I insisted that she had actually done him a *favor* by helping him launch his program.

I also went to Brooklyn for the retiring Dwyane Wade's farewell on the last night of the 2018–19 regular season. I always loved Wade's stylish game, just as you did. It turned into one of those impromptu NBA "events" you loved so much. LeBron showed up to support his buddy, as did Carmelo. Mr. Miami, Pat Riley, was there, tanned and dapper as ever at seventy-four. The game ended at 10:30. Wade addressed the media at 11:15. Got home at midnight.

Finished a column at 3:30 A.M. Woke up at 6:15 to edit it.
Filed at 7 A.M. Spent the next two days in recovery, hearing
my father's voice asking me: *What do you need it for?* And with
yours countering: *It's not what you need. It's what you want.*

Michelle, I have to tell you that I will always feel selfish for
having complained to you about feeling *left out* from covering
the 2018 playoffs at a time you already knew or at least
suspected you were dying. You had every right to be annoyed,
even angry. But I also realize now that when you scolded me
for sulking you weren't telling me never to write again—just
not to agonize over the inactivity and the inevitable transition
to the career afterlife. To regard the possibility of being
professionally idle not as punishment, but as reward. To not
correlate career closure as a prelude to life's conclusion.

I suppose the work drug isn't the worst way to self-
medicate as we age—though I am trying to keep in mind the
adage you occasionally invoked that nobody on their deathbed
ever wished they had spent more time at the office. I still
don't want to be that person who regrets clinging to what I
know and have already done. And while I'd like to believe I
have years remaining to explore, to find that place of personal
contentment—as you did for a good spell—sixty-seven is the
age at which my father died, exactly my age in 2019. So, yes,
even before the pandemic, mortality had been on my mind.

You often said that people use their careers to avoid the
mere contemplation of it, to preoccupy themselves in the
whirlwind of the workweek while convincing themselves
that being needed at the office means they are still in a vital
stage of life. My eye condition, of course, works as an

effective rejoinder. Fortunately, Frank Bruni continues to write columns about coping with his sight challenges, including one about a man who lost his vision and proceeded to publish his first novel! I find these columns to be uplifting, even therapeutic. And while I can't help but occasionally fret over the likelihood of a blurry future, my condition also forces me to relish what I have each and every day and to think about *how* I wish to spend however much quality time—or any kind of time—I have left.

I have to admit that as a younger man I would look at the elderly and wonder how they even motivated themselves to get through a day, much less be happy, knowing they had already lived the majority of their lives. Then I watched you throughout your retirement years and especially during the uncertainty and limitations of your final year. Until your very last days, you made the most of each one, relished every hour at yoga, or with a friend (like me!), or in front of the television with LeBron and Durant. What an example you set by refusing to let go of the life you loved—until you stared down its end with such calm resolve.

Which reminds me: In late March of 2019, three weeks before the Knicks' season ended, we lost yet another eminent Garden elder. Cal Ramsey passed—like you, at eighty-one. I know how fond you were of him, one of your section buddies, part of the Willis Reed crowd that you ran with back in the eighties, when the whole scene was new and exciting and your great escape from suburban boredom.

Just as your children did for you, Cal's people held a wonderful celebration of his life, though there was one downer moment during the service that would have made you cringe. It was when the hostess asked for the prearranged speakers to step forward and mentioned them by name: a cousin of Cal's; the retired Harlem congressman Charles Rangel; and a man who needed no introduction, James Dolan.

Heads turned. There was a collective gasp and you could almost hear people thinking, *Dolan is here?* Alas, for whatever reason, it turned out he wasn't, and apparently hadn't bothered to inform anyone—at least not in time—that he would be unable to speak, or attend. When his name was called a second time with no response, it was awkward, embarrassing, infuriating. A former NBA league office employee, sitting next to me, shook his head and whispered, "Big surprise."

Plenty of basketball people from the Knicks organization, the league, and the greater New York basketball community did show, though. I won't name them all, but you couldn't miss Charles Oakley's speckled head of gray a few rows ahead of mine. And right next to Oak sat Charles Smith. In other words, Michelle, you chose your Garden friends well. And you, like Cal, were part of that greater family there not defined by the likes of its chairman—the people's Garden. Oakley and Smith and all the others could count on you to be there for them, to not boo or abandon them when they inevitably came up short in a playoff game, or any game.

As for your Knicks, they wound up using all the salary cap space they'd created in the Porzingis trade by signing (and overpaying) a bunch of B- and C-list veteran free agents to short-term deals, hoping to provide mentorship to Barrett and their other young players. And also, I suppose, to win a few games, try to make a run at the 2020 playoffs after years of misery and tanking. The television network crowd didn't seem too convinced. When the 2019 Christmas Day lineup of games was announced, the Knicks weren't on it, a rare omission that spoke volumes about how far they had fallen. By the 2020 All-Star break, they had canned another coach, dumped another team president, hired a self-proclaimed branding guru, and tabbed Carmelo's agent—no, *really*—as chief basketball executive.

On the night the agent-turned-president, Leon Rose, attended his first game, Spike Lee just happened to argue with Garden security over which entrance he could use—and that turned into a very public dispute between Spike and Dolan's PR minions. Though he wasn't handcuffed or carried out, like Oak, his takeaway quote echoed you, Michelle, in summing up the sad state of the loyal Knicks fan—celebrity or civilian—in the Dolan era. More plea than complaint, Spike whined to a reporter: "Am I going to go to the grave without another banner being raised in the world's most famous arena?"

But who knows? Maybe in the post-pandemic world they will finally have the kind of patience Brooklyn had in nurturing Barrett and their promising young talent and perhaps then the Garden will become an attractive landing spot for an actual superstar, as Barclays Center became for the Nets. During the run-up to the 2019 summer free agency, I actually had begun to wonder how I would deal with the jubilation of the fan base if they did score big, the excitement of the nineties returned, and the Knicks somehow won the championship that never happened on your front-row watch:

Would I resent it because it came too late for you, who deserved it as much as any fan who ever pushed through a Garden turnstile? Or would that be overstating the value of results, giving too much credibility to the all-or-nothing mentality that is so pervasive in (sigh) newspaper columns and on sports talk radio?

I'm not suggesting that winning is not the point of competing and not worth celebrating, and I know you never would either. But at least from the pragmatic fan's point of view, I have come to wonder if those championship banners hanging from the rafters are even transferrable in emotional value from one generation to the next, or ultimately are more like the souvenir game notes, ticket stubs, and assorted *stuff* your kids predictably tossed. If we learned anything during the no-sports pandemic of 2020, morosely watching reruns of games from years past and wondering if it would ever be safe enough to go back to a crowded public space, including the Garden, it should have been what I suspected you always understood: the emotional connection was far more about the journey than it was the trophy.

I do have one keepsake from your condo: the photo taken of us at NASA's Space Center gift shop in Houston during the 1994 Finals. It hangs in my home office now. When I look at it, I invariably find myself thinking about the night of Game 7—the Starks shooting nightmare—and recalling how you surprised me when you rejected Riley's winning-and-misery maxim and insisted you would have no lasting regrets that the Knicks had lost. If others preferred to cast blame and be bitter, you, conversely, were inclined to applaud them because they had, as you always put it, *shown up* every night, just as you had. That, you said, was invariably all you could ask—of them, and especially of us.

I also have to tell you that I returned to the Hall of Fame in Springfield in early September 2019 to support Marc Stein, who was the recipient of the same Curt Gowdy Media Award I'd received two years earlier. Even though he'd only been at the *Times* for a fairly short while after a lengthy run at ESPN, the editors graciously bought a table, as they did for me. His speech was excellent—polished, smart. But wouldn't you know it? *He* had the benefit of a teleprompter! No complaints, though. I know I had a better guide to help me get through my speech without screwing it up. I had you! I was blessed.

In the final analysis, I guess we all have the glass-half-full option in any subjective evaluation. Thank you for helping me to understand that, for making me think harder about my work and my world. For all the laughs and life lessons. For the lasting reminders to live each day with purpose. To focus on the gift of each day. To appreciate, above all, the special people.

Of all the great things that happened for me at Madison Square Garden over the past four decades, and there were many, our friendship was truly the best and most profitable of all. And if I didn't clearly see that, I would have to have been closed to the core, blind in the worst possible way.

With love and appreciation, always,
Harvey

Acknowledgments

On several occasions, Michelle and I discussed my writing about our love of the game through the prism of our decades-long friendship. In later years, we even recorded a few of our marathon dinner conversations. We never actually thought such a project would happen, if only because books are so much easier to conceptualize than to create, and on top of that, we relished our shared time much too much to burden it with, well, work.

Life inevitably got in the way, and then illness, and then death. And while writing Michelle's obituary in the *New York Times* seemed at the time like the perfect tribute to her, her other friends, hearing about the book idea, would in so many words tell me I absolutely had to do it. I believe that they—and ultimately I—envisioned it as a way to keep her with us for that much longer.

While I was still mourning Michelle, my smart, steadfast agent, Andrew Blauner, helped me to distill my emotions into a more focused written proposal. He connected me with Scott Moyers and Emily Cunningham at Penguin Press, which allowed me the privilege of working with Emily, an extraordinary editor who recognized far sooner than I how this project needed to proceed and whose patient, meticulous guidance was so instrumental in its completion. Thanks to Colleen Boyle, Daniel Novack, Shina Patel, and others at Penguin Press, as well as to Kym Surridge, for their roles in making this book happen.

To Drucie De Vries, Lori Hamamoto, Jay Greenberg, Robin Kelly, Ernestine Miller, and Wynn Plaut, Michelle's other MSG besties—thank you for sharing with me so generously. She loved you all.

Confronting such personal issues—Michelle's and my own—was not easy many mornings. My Sandwich Theory breakfast crowd in Montclair took precious time from solving the problems of the world to hear about my challenges before sending me back to my laptop, determined to move forward. Thank you, Joseph Bertolotti, Robert Cumins, Michelle Fine, Joe Fortunato, Dennis Johnston, Ed Martin, Suzanne Moyers, A. J. Savastinuk, Jane Seaman, Susan and Miles Tepper, Sandy Sorkin, and David Surrey.

Thanks to my longtime "locals," Filip Bondy, Dave Kaplan, Rich Kopilnick, and Mitch Greene, and to confidants Howard Blatt, Selena Roberts, Barry Stanton, and Lloyd Stone. A nod to my basketball journalism brethren, Howard Beck, Scott Cacciola, Marc Stein, Adrian Wojnarowski, and Ailene Voisin; and a shout-out to all the editors at the *New York Times*, *Daily News*, *New York Post*, and *Staten Island Advance* who had my back through the years.

To Roy Johnson, Dave Sims, Kevin Kernan, and the late Paul Needell—a salute for sharing the space around Michelle's seat back in the day.

I owe a huge debt of gratitude to Michelle's children, Brandon, Bruce, Darcy, Devon, and Blair. Your contributions here were deeply meaningful. Your family will forever be special to me.

At home, there has never been any shortage of love and support from my amazing wife, Beth, and my sons, Alex and Charly, of whom I am so proud. Michelle often lectured me on how blessed I am. As with most things, she was so right.

Index